NATIONS *IN TRANSITION*

IRAN

New and future titles in the
Nations in Transition series include:

China

India

Indonesia

Ireland

North Korea

Pakistan

Russia

South Korea

Vietnam

NATIONS *IN TRANSITION*

IRAN

by Charles Clark

GREENHAVEN PRESS
SAN DIEGO, CALIFORNIA

THOMSON
━━━━✦━━━ ™
GALE

Detroit • New York • San Diego • San Francisco
Boston • New Haven, Conn. • Waterville, Maine
London • Munich

Library of Congress Cataloging-in-Publication Data

Iran / by Charles Clark.
    p. cm. — (Nations in transition)
Includes bibliographical references and index.
Summary: Examines the history of Iran from ancient times to the
present, life before and after the Islamic Revolution, the current state
of affairs, and Iran's place in the world today.
ISBN 0-7377-1096-9
1. Iran. I. Clark, Charles, 1949– . II. Title. III. Series:
Nations in transition (Greenhaven Press)
    DS272.C37 2002
    955—dc21

                                                    2002001266

Copyright © 2002 by Greenhaven Press,
an imprint of The Gale Group
10911 Technology Place, San Diego, CA 92127
Printed in the U.S.A.

Contents

Foreword

In 1986 Soviet general secretary Mikhail Gorbachev initiated his plan to reform the economic, political, and social structure of the Soviet Union. Nearly three-quarters of a century of Communist ideology was dismantled in the next five years. As the totalitarian regime relaxed its rule and opened itself up to the West, the Soviet peoples clamored for more freedoms. Hard-line Communists resisted Gorbachev's lead, but glasnost, or "openness," could not be stopped with the will of the common people behind it.

In 1991 the changing USSR held its first multicandidate elections. The reform-minded Boris Yeltsin, a supporter of Gorbachev, became the first popularly elected president of the Russian Republic in Soviet history. Under Yeltsin's leadership, the old Communist policies soon all but disintegrated, as did the Soviet Union itself. The Union of Soviet Socialist Republics broke apart into fifteen independent entities. The former republics reformed into a more democratic union now referred to as the Commonwealth of Independent States. Russia remained the nominal figurehead of the commonwealth, but it no longer dictated the future of the other independent states.

By the new millennium, Russia and the other commonwealth states still faced crises. The new states were all in transition from decades of totalitarian rule to the postglasnost era of unprecedented and untested democratic reforms. Revamping the Soviet economy may have opened up new opportunities in private ownership of property and business, but it did not bring overnight prosperity to the former republics. Common necessities such as food still remain in short supply in many regions. And while new governments seek to stabilize their authority, crime rates have escalated throughout the former Soviet Union. Still, the people are confident that their newfound freedoms—freedom of speech and assembly, freedom of religion, and even the right of workers to strike—will ultimately better their lives. The process of change will take time and the people are willing to see their respective states through the challenges of this transitional period in Soviet history.

The collapse and rebuilding of the former Soviet Union provides perhaps the best example of a contemporary "nation in transition," the focus of this Greenhaven Press series. However, other nations that fall under the series rubric have faced a host of unique and varied cultural shifts. India, for instance, is a stable, guiding force in Asia, yet it remains a nation in transition more than fifty years after winning independence from Great Britain. The entire infrastructure of the Indian subcontinent still bears the marking of its colonial past: In a land of eighteen official spoken languages, for example, English remains the voice of politics and education. India is still coming to grips with its colonial legacy while forging its place as a strong player in Asian and world affairs.

North Korea's place in Greenhaven's Nations in Transition series is based on major recent political developments. After decades of antagonism between its Communist government and the democratic leadership of South Korea, tensions seemed to ease in the late 1990s. Even under the shadow of the North's developing nuclear capabilities, the presidents of both North and South Korea met in 2000 to propose plans for possible reunification of the two estranged nations. And though it is one of the three remaining bastions of communism in the world, North Korea is choosing not to remain an isolated relic of the Cold War. While it has not earned the trust of the United States and many of its Western allies, North Korea has begun to reach out to its Asian neighbors to encourage trade and cultural exchanges.

These three countries exemplify the types of changes and challenges that qualify them as subjects of study in the Greenhaven Nations in Transition series. The series examines specific nations to disclose the major social, political, economic, and cultural shifts that have caused massive change and in many cases, brought about regional and/or worldwide shifts in power. Detailed maps, inserts, and pictures help flesh out the people, places, and events that define the country's transitional period. Furthermore, a comprehensive bibliography points readers to other sources that will deepen their understanding of the nation's complex past and contemporary struggles. With these tools, students and casual readers trace both past history and future challenges of these important nations.

Introduction
The Changing Face of Iran

The years 1978 and 1979 were convulsive for Iran. What became known as the Islamic Revolution changed Iran dramatically and affected many other countries around the world as well. Journalist Robin Wright, who visited Iran many times both before and after the Islamic Revolution, contends that the revolution was one of the twentieth century's turning points. She says that only two other events during the century had a similar impact on the Middle East: the collapse of the Ottoman Empire in 1922, which set the stage for the creation of nations such as Turkey and Iraq, and the creation of the state of Israel in 1948.

Iran's Islamic Revolution has made an impact outside the Middle East. The nation's internal turmoil increased world oil prices—Iran has been a major oil-producing nation since the early twentieth century, and control of the nation's oil has often been a focus for international conflict. The revolution also sparked an eight-year war between Iran and Iraq, contributed to an increase in global terrorism, and made people worldwide more aware of the role religion plays in political conflict.

Today, over two decades after the revolution, Iran is unique. It has combined elements of several forms of government. In addition, in a region where civil rights are often severely limited, Iran has managed to have vigorous public debates about a range of issues. As Wright explains,

> Although thoroughly Islamic with several unique twists, Iran has become a modern republic based on a unique blend of Islamic and European law, most notably borrowing ideas from France and Belgium. It calls for national, provincial and local elections in which all males and females vote as of age fifteen. It stipulates term limits for the presidency and

allocates parliamentary seats for Christians, Jews and Zoroastrians—at least token acknowledgment of individual minority rights.[1]

The Global Reach of the Revolution

The Iranian revolution and the government it produced also had a larger impact. Since the leaders of the Islamic Republic considered many neighboring Muslim countries heretical, corrupt, or both, they wanted these nations to have their own revolutions and create governments based on the Iranian model. Other nations in the region, such as Saudi Arabia and the United Arab Emirates, have majority-Muslim populations and governments that are at least nominally guided by Islamic principles, but Iran was the first modern Shii theocracy, that is, a government based on the pattern presented by Shii Islam and headed by Muslim clerics. Iran's revolution inspired Shii fervor throughout the Middle East. The result was a new round

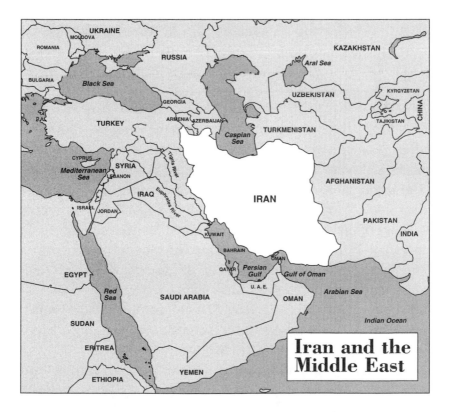

Iran and the Middle East

of political turmoil and violence. According to journalist Sandra Mackey:

> As the Islamic Republic in perception and reality pushed the revolution beyond the borders of Iran, the West moved to contain it. To the detriment of both, the forces of revolution and the forces of containment met in Lebanon. In April 1983, the American embassy on Bliss Street crumbled in the fire and force of a bomb delivered in a van by the Iranian-inspired Islamic Jihad. Militants from Lebanon's Shia Muslim population dispatched two more bombs on a quiet Sunday morning the following October. One massacred 241 United States Marines, the other 47 soldiers of the French contingent of the Multinational Force sent to Lebanon in a misguided attempt to restore order to a country ravaged by its own civil war and the 1982 Israeli invasion. Three months later, in February 1984, groups gathered under the umbrella of a shadowy organization called Hezbollah began to snatch Americans and Europeans off the streets of Lebanon. By January 1987, Hezbollah, possessing undefined but discernible ties to Iran, held hostage the nationals of the United States, Britain, France, Ireland, and the Federal Republic of Germany.[2]

Iran's size, potential wealth, and strategic location make its internal politics and foreign policy vitally important to the United States and other nations. During the Cold War, when the United States and the Soviet Union jockeyed for strategic advantage in the Middle East and Asia, Iran figured prominently in the foreign policies of both superpowers. The United States had much more influence in Iran before the Islamic Revolution because of its strong economic and military ties to the government of the Iranian king, Muhammad Reza Shah Pahlavi. Then the revolution heightened U.S. fears of greater Soviet influence, though in fact the revolution's leader, Ayatollah Khomeini, was vehemently opposed to both the United States and the Soviet Union.

In the years since the Islamic Revolution, Iran has remained at odds with the West, particularly the United States, on many fronts. Iran also continues to have major internal problems: political unrest, a weak economy, widespread pollution, underfunded and understaffed hospitals and schools, and crumbling roads and bridges, to name just a few. But Iran also possesses surprising strengths. The ways in which Iran's people cope with the challenges of the twenty-first century may well have implications not only for their nation but also for the world at large.

Iran Before the Islamic Revolution

1

The modern nation of Iran is the successor to the ancient nation of Persia. For most of its history, Persia was governed by kings who believed that God had made it possible for them to rule. The Persian people took this to mean that their rulers should govern fairly and try to establish a just society based on divine law. Thus, the Persian—and Iranian—approach to governance has always included the principle that no ruler should have absolute authority but should be guided by the ethical norms of religion.

Persia in the Age of Empire

Modern Iran traces its cultural roots to the Persian Empire, which rose approximately twenty-five hundred years ago. Two tribes, the Medes and the Persians, had shared the vast Iranian Plateau for a thousand years. The Medes dominated the region until about 550 B.C., when Cyrus the Great became king of the Persians. Cyrus conquered the Medes, as well as the neighboring Lydians and Babylonians, extending his rule far beyond the bounds of Persia and establishing the Achaemenian Empire, the largest in the world at that time. Cyrus's successors—Cambyses, Darius, and Xerxes—were also adept military leaders, so that during Xerxes' reign the Persian Empire encompassed almost 2 million square miles, stretching from Egypt to India and from the northern shores of the Arabian Sea to the southern shores of the Caspian and Black Seas.

Under Persian rule, civilization in the region flourished. According to authors Pat Yale, Anthony Ham, and Paul Greenway:

> At the height of their power the Achaemenids ruled over one of the greatest of early civilisations. Paved roads suitable for

horse-drawn carriages stretched from one end of their empire to the other, with caravanserais [inns] at regular intervals to provide food and shelter to travellers. The Achaemenids are also credited with having introduced the world's first courier service for transmitting mail around their territories.[3]

The Persians were known for their high culture and efficient administration, but their vast empire was not destined to last. Rebellions arose in a number of their provinces, but the Greeks were the principal source of trouble for the Persians. In 331 B.C., after a three-year campaign, the Persian Empire was conquered by the Greek king, Alexander the Great. Alexander continued to expand his empire for several more years. When he died in 323, a battle ensued among his generals for control of his empire. One of the victors was Seleucus, who established a dynasty that ruled Persia for two hundred years. The Seleucid dynasty was in turn overthrown in the second century B.C. by the Parthians, a formerly nomadic people who had migrated south along the east coast of the

Enameled bricks depict the Royal Persian guard. The Persians were known for their high culture and efficient administration.

Caspian Sea and into Persia at the end of Alexander's reign. The Parthian dynasty controlled Persia for four hundred years, defeating attempted Roman invasions.

Ardashir, a provincial king, rebelled against the Parthians in A.D. 224 and established the Sassanid dynasty. Ardashir made Zoroastrianism, which had begun in Persia seven hundred years earlier, the official religion of the empire.

Islamic Rule

The rule of Persia by Persians came to an end in 651 when, after fifteen years of fighting, the Persian Empire was overwhelmed by the Arabs, who brought not only a ruling military elite but a new religion, Islam. A new age had begun, and though Persian language and culture never disappeared completely, Islam would thereafter be the dominant religious and cultural force in Iran.

The coming of the Arabs and Islam was not a severe hardship for many Persians. The Muslims regarded the Zoroastrians, Jews, and Christians of Persia as *ahl al-Kitab,* the "People of the Book," meaning that they had received and followed previous revelations from God and should be respected for that. Persia actually proved to be fertile soil for Islam because the concepts of justice and of kings ruling by the will of God are shared by Zoroastrianism and Islam. Moreover, according to religion scholar John Esposito, Judaism, Christianity, and Zoroastrianism

> shared a monotheistic faith (the conviction that God is one), prophets, Scriptures, beliefs in angels and devils, and a moral universe encompassing individual and communal accountability and responsibility. All were the product of primarily urban, not rural or desert experiences, and were institutionalized in commercial centers by scholarly elites, often supported by state patronage, who interpreted the early teaching of their prophets and apostles. Among their common themes were community, fidelity/infidelity, individual moral decision making, social justice, final judgment, and reward and punishment.[4]

The Rise of Islam

Islam, the religion that in time came to pervade all aspects of life in Persia, began in the early seventh century in the Arab city of Mecca. A man named Muhammad began to receive what he believed were revelations from God commanding him to tell his people to abandon their old way of life. The Arabs worshiped many gods, though most believed there was a high God, Allah. The message Muhammad received was that God had no equals and no partners, that the other gods were false, and that God now required people to submit to his will. The way of life that God commanded was partly spelled out in the revelations Muhammad received and partly through the example of Muhammad himself, who was regarded as the perfect man because of his perfect submission to the will of God. The religion became known as Islam, the Arabic word for "submission," and its followers are Muslims, those who submit.

The revelations Muhammad received became the holy book of Islam, the Quran. Islam acknowledges that people other than the Arabs had previously received valid revelations from God that had been recorded in holy books: the Jews in the Torah, the Christians in the Gospels, and the Zoroastrians in their scripture, the Zend Avesta. The Allah of Islam is the same God worshiped by Jews, Christians, and Zoroastrians.

Over the next three hundred years, Islam became the religion of virtually all Persians. The branch of Islam that dominated in Iran changed over time, however. The Islam that first came to Persia is now known as Sunni Islam. It is the branch of the faith to which the majority of Muslims belonged. In Sunni Islam, there is a division between political and religious authority. The Sunnis hold that Muhammad's successors were the caliphs, who assumed only one of the roles of Muhammad, that of political leader of the Muslim community. The Sunnis vested religious authority in the religious scholars, known as the ulema, men who had studied the Quran and the example set by Muhammad. The ulema were considered capable of rendering judgments about personal conduct and were qualified to advise their rulers on public policy. In Sunni Islam, the caliph was expected to seek the opinion of the community of Muslim scholars when making important decisions so that they would be in accord with the principles of Islam.

But another branch of Islam, the Shia, increased in importance in Iran over the centuries. Shia Islam began because when Muhammad died, it was unclear who should be his successor. The majority of his close companions chose Muhammad's friend Abu Bakr as caliph, but a minority insisted that only Muhammad's closest male relative, Ali ibn Abi Talib, could succeed him. Ali was finally chosen as the fourth caliph, but his rule was disputed. A bitter and bloody split developed between his supporters (the *shia* or party of Ali) and the supporters of his rival, Muawiyyah. Ali was killed, and later his sons and successors, Hasan and Hussein, were also martyred. The Shia called Ali, his sons, and those who came after them imams, or leaders. Some of the Shia thought there were seven legitimate imams following Muhammad's death. Others thought there were twelve, and eventually this group, known as the Twelver Shia, became dominant in Persia.

Shia Islam first became the official religion of Persia in the sixteenth century. According to journalist Sandra Mackey,

> Iranians . . . accepted Shiism as an integral part of Iranian identity because it spoke to Persian culture and the Iranian experience. From the first century of Islam, the martyrdom of Ali and Hussein held particular meaning for Iranians. . . . Iranians saw in the Shia martyrs shadows of themselves. For they too were a defeated and humiliated people whose rights and deepest convictions had been trampled. But even more, Ali provided the Iranians with their archetypal model for political order—the just ruler. In a parallel with Persian kingship, the Iranians accepted the cause of Ali and the house of the Prophet because it coincided with their pre-Islamic traditions of legitimacy.[5]

The Safavid Dynasty

The ruler who established Shia Islam as the official religion of Persia was Shah Esma'il I. He was the first of the Safavid shahs, a dynasty named after Esma'il's ancestor Sheik Safi.

The Safavid shahs were principally concerned with their neighbors to the west, the powerful Ottoman Empire. For over a hundred years, the two empires frequently warred over control of present-day Iraq. The Safavids captured the Iraqi capital of Baghdad in 1509, lost it in 1523, regained it in 1534, and lost it again (and permanently) in 1638. This period of conflict served to solidify the control of the Safavid dynasty and Shia Islam because justifications for the wars were often cast in religious terms: Persia's opponents, the Ottomans, were Sunni Muslims, so the wars were a continuation of the centuries-old rivalry between Sunni and Shia.

After the final loss of Iraq to the Ottomans, Persia experienced a period of relative peace and prosperity. The Safavid shahs built a magnificent new capital city at Esfahan in central Persia, and they initiated trade in carpets and textiles with Europe, especially Britain. One result of the prosperity, though, was that the Safavid rulers increasingly adopted lavish lifestyles that drained the national treasury. Safavid shahs tended to be so afraid of conspiracies against them that they executed anyone who might become a threat, including other members of the royal family. Persia became

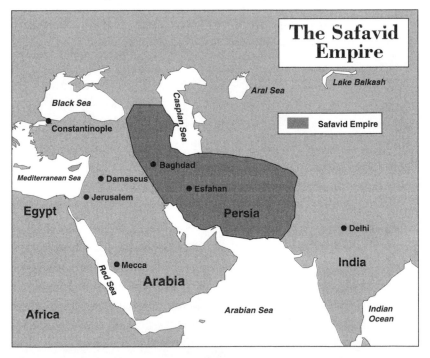

progressively weaker under the Safavids; when the Afghans invaded in 1722, they were able to march to Esfahan and execute the last of the Safavid shahs, Sultan Husayn.

The Qajar Dynasty and the Constitutional Revolution

Following the end of the Safavid dynasty, Persia suffered from seventy years of civil unrest. For a time, Russian and Ottoman forces occupied parts of the country. Though the foreigners were forced out within a few years, no leader was able to both unify the nation and provide stable rule. Then in 1794 Agha Muhammad Khan, a warlord from the Azeri region in northern Persia, defeated competing tribal leaders and established the Qajar dynasty, becoming known as Agha Muhammad Shah. He soon died and was succeeded by his nephew, Fath 'Ali Shah, who tried to reestablish the extravagances of the ancient Persian court.

There were many sources of discontent with Qajar rule among the Persian people. The power of the Muslim clergy had been limited during the period of crisis and chaos, but now that there was relative peace, they began to ask for more authority and a larger role for Islam in public life. The clerics were generally unable to influence government policies, however. The last two Qajar shahs of the nineteenth century, Naser od-Din Shah, who ruled from 1848 to 1896, and Mozaffar od-Din Shah, who ruled from 1896 to 1907, ran up huge debts, mostly in pursuit of their own comfort and amusement. Many Persians thought that the Qajars weakened their country's sovereignty when they handed over control of much of the economy to the British, who had long sought to increase their power in the region. The Qajars also seemed helpless to deal with the military threats posed by the Russian conquest of Central Asia and Britain's control of Afghanistan.

In the end, however, pressure from religious authorities brought an end to Qajar rule. For example, in 1891 the government sold the British the right to buy the entire Iranian tobacco crop. This decision provoked a storm of protest. Muslim scholars issued a decree that the sale was illegal under Islamic law, and a strike was led by Islamic clergy in which tobacco growers and dealers stopped work,

This nineteenth-century tile shows Naser od-Din Shah hunting. He was one of the last Qajar shahs.

paralyzing the industry and cutting off a major source of the shah's income. The protests and the economic effects of the strike forced the shah to withdraw the sale.

A similar dispute arose in 1905 when the government tried to manipulate sugar prices. Iranian merchants, however, believed that their marketplace system of setting prices was ordained by God. When two sugar merchants in Tehran refused to cooperate, the government punished them by having them beaten on the soles of their feet. Again the clergy led protests and a massive strike that forced the government to relent, not only on the issue of sugar but also on the protesters' larger demand for a written constitution limiting royal power and for the creation of a *majlis,* an elected assembly. The shah stalled implementation of the reforms, but after another round of protests, in 1906 a constitution was drawn up and an assembly was elected. The nation retained a Qajar ruler in name only, Sultan Ahmed Shah, who was a boy when he became king in 1907 and never functioned as an effective ruler.

Reza Shah Pahlavi

The changes brought about by the 1906 revolution, however, were not sufficient to produce the orderly government and prosperous economy the reformers hoped for. For one thing, the central government proved too weak to keep order. The Russians were able to strengthen their influence in northern Iran to the extent that Russian troops attacked the Majlis building in 1911, forcing the assembly to disband. The experiment in democracy begun by the Constitutional Revolution had failed. With a weak shah who was unable to maintain order, the countryside fell ever more deeply into chaos, being ruled by local warlords. The man who imposed order on the chaos was Reza Khan, commander of one of the more effective units of the army, the Cossack Brigade. He defeated the warlords, drove out foreign troops, and put down rebellions by ethnic minorities. By February 1921, Reza Khan was the most influential man in Iran, even though Sultan Ahmed Shah still held the Qajar throne.

Reza Khan, first shah of the Pahlavi dynasty.

By 1925, Reza Khan had consolidated his power, and the nation was at a crossroads. The choice seemed to be between a secular republic with Reza as head of state or to keep the monarchy with Reza as the first shah of a new dynasty. Persia's Muslim clergy feared they would lose power under a secular republic, so they urged the Majlis to depose Sultan Ahmed and make Reza Khan the new king of Persia. Reza established the Pahlavi dynasty, adopting the name of the ancient language of Persia so that it would seem that he was reviving pre-Islamic Persian culture. Many Persians regarded Reza Shah Pahlavi as a strongman capable of maintaining order and stability so that the nation would have a chance to recover from decades of turmoil. His strict autocratic rule was welcomed because he guaranteed peace in the streets and in the bazaar, allowing commerce to function normally again.

Even though the Muslim clergy had been instrumental in making him king, Reza Shah wanted to limit their power. He modeled his policies on those of the Turkish ruler Mustafa Kemal Atatürk, a secularist who believed that Turkey could not become part of the modern world unless the influence of Islam lessened. Atatürk believed that the Islamic clergy would oppose his reforms, especially those designed to improve relations with Europe. Just as Atatürk had done in Turkey, Reza Shah reduced the power of the Islamic clergy, repealed laws based on the Islamic system of justice, and required that the Persian people dress in Western clothes.

To emphasize his break with the past, in 1935 Reza changed the name of his nation to Iran. Reza also began to modernize Iran by building bridges, railways, schools, and hospitals. Although many of his projects were successful in the short term, they caused as many problems as they solved. Substantial elements of Iranian society, especially the clergy, wanted nothing new that would interfere with traditional Islamic ways. They resented having to wear Western clothing, and the withdrawal of funding from mosques and *madrassahs* (Islamic colleges) made it difficult for the clergy to function.

When some Iranians protested against his policies, Reza used his military to suppress dissent. He silenced those who spoke out against him—then imprisoned, exiled, or even executed them. The Muslim clergy, however, were not willing to let the role of Islam in Iran be abolished. They did not advocate overthrowing the shah, but they mobilized around issues on which they felt the shah was betraying Islam, such as abandoning the Islamic legal system in favor of one based on European law. According to historian Roy Mottahedeh, in July 1935,

> angry crowds thronged into the courtyard of the shrine in Mashhad, . . . for the Shiah [Shia] the holiest spot in Iran. They came to hear preachers attack the policies of Reza Shah. When they did not disperse, Reza Shah's troops mounted machine

guns on the roofs overlooking the courtyard and opened fire. Over one hundred people were killed. Three soldiers who had refused to fire were shot. No further hostile religious demonstrations of any significance took place in Reza Shah's reign.[6]

Just as Reza did not want to share power with the mullahs (Muslim clerics), he did not want to share it with the British. The British were entitled to a large portion of the revenue from the oil industry, which reduced the amount Iran retained to fund its government. In the 1930s, Reza tried to limit British influence by hiring German technical staff to run the oil fields. But when Britain and Germany went to war in 1939, the British feared the German workers would sabotage the oil fields. To prevent this, the British told Reza to expel the Germans. He refused. The situation remained unresolved until 1941, when the Soviet Union entered the war against Germany. British and Soviet troops invaded Iran and sent Reza into exile.

Muhammad Reza Pahlavi

The British wanted to keep the oil fields secure and protect their military interests, but they did not want to rule Iran directly. They put Reza's son Muhammad on the throne with the understanding that he would respect the constitution. Then in 1942 the United States also sent troops to guard the nation's railroads. The new shah, Muhammad Reza Pahlavi, appeared ready to allow the Iranian people more democratic freedoms. He allowed the 1944 parliamentary elections to go forward without interference; the campaign for the election gave a range of political groups a voice for the first time in two decades.

Still, what many saw as the excessive influence of foreign nations dominated the political landscape. In particular, the status of the oil industry was a sore point. A British company, the Anglo-Iranian Oil Company (AIOC), still owned the rights to all of Iran's crude oil, and though they paid a yearly fee based on production, much more of the revenue from oil sales went to Britain than to Iran. For example, in 1950 AIOC paid $45 million in fees to Iran but $142 million in taxes to Britain. Many Iranians were outraged at this and wanted to nationalize the oil industry—that is, to cancel the agreement with Britain, run the oil industry directly, and keep all the income from sales. They got their wish in 1951 when the leader of the nationalization movement, Muhammad Mosaddeq, became the nation's prime minister. Mosaddeq, a lawyer and aristocrat, was the leader of the National Front, a coalition of parties opposed to the shah's policies. According to journalist and biographer Baqer Moin, "Mosaddeq had an impeccable reputation for honesty and public service. With his charismatic personality and unique political style he was able to mobilise mass popular support both for the nationalization of Iran's British-owned oil industry and for his attempts to limit the Shah's powers."[7]

Mosaddeq nationalized the oil industry, saying that Iran would become self-sufficient. To emphasize his point, he sent home all the

---

Veiling

The compulsory veiling of women has long been a controversial topic in Iran. In 1935, twenty years before Shah Muhammad Reza Pahlavi outlawed the wearing of the veil in public, Taj al-Saltana, the liberal-minded daughter of one of the last Qajar shahs, called for veiling to end. An advocate of women's rights, she believed that the segregation of women, as symbolized by the veil, kept her country from economic prosperity. In her autobiography, *Crowning Anguish: Memoirs of a Persian Princess from the Harem to Modernity*, she explains her views.

> The source of the ruination of the country, the cause of its moral laxity, the obstacle to its advancement in all areas, is the veiling of women. Owing to fatalities, the number of men in Persia is always smaller than that of women. In a country where two-thirds of its population [that is, women] has to remain idle at home, the remaining third has to exert itself to the utmost to provide the comforts, sustenance and clothing for the others. So they cannot attend to the affairs of the nation and its progress. Now if these two-thirds were employed in meaningful work, the nation would make two-fold progress, and everyone would be wealthy.

British technical staff who had been running the oil fields. The shah, whose political power was at a low point, could only sit by helplessly and watch events unfold. Britain retaliated against the nationalization by blockading oil shipments, and the Iranians soon found that they lacked the technical expertise to operate the oil fields and pipelines. Revenues plummeted, and Iran was again in an economic and political crisis. Mosaddeq appealed for assistance to U.S. president Dwight Eisenhower, citing the possibility that Iran might be taken over by the Iranian Communist Party with the help of the Soviet Union. Instead of agreeing to strengthen Mosaddeq, whom Eisenhower considered unreliable, in August 1953 the United States engineered a coup in which Mosaddeq was removed from office. U.S. officials agreed with Mosaddeq that the Soviets might take over Iran as a result of the crisis, but they thought Muhammad Reza Shah was likely to be more effective in dealing with this threat.

The shah had fled Iran during the crisis. He soon returned, however, and with U.S. backing established a more authoritarian government than in his first twelve years as king. While Reza Shah initiated some reforms and industrialization projects, just as his father had, he tended to act without regard to the views of the Iranian people. Many Iranians saw Reza Shah as a puppet controlled by foreign interests (the United States chief among them, thanks to its role in the removal of Prime Minister Mosaddeq).

The Origins of the Islamic Revolution

Many Iranians thought that Muhammad Reza Shah was more concerned about pleasing foreign governments than about the welfare of his own people. They cited his cooperation with foreign oil companies, his agreement to allow foreign troops on Iranian soil, and his attempts to diminish the role of Islam in public life. For example, in October 1962 the shah proposed a bill to give women the vote and to allow non-Muslim candidates to run for public office.

Ayatollah Ruhollah Khomeini, a Muslim cleric and leader of the opposition, argued that both proposals violated Islamic law. He said at the time, "The son of Reza Khan has embarked on the destruction of Islam in Iran. I will oppose this as long as the blood

Ayatollah Khomeini

As a young man Ayatollah Khomeini traveled to Sultanabad (present-day Arak), to study Islamic law under a renowned teacher, Sheik Abdolkarim Ha'eri. When Ha'eri moved to Qom in 1922, Khomeini followed him. There, he studied theology, philosophy, and Islamic law and rose from pupil to ayatollah, the highest rank of a Shiite cleric. At a time when many clerics purposely dressed in worn-out robes made of rough cloth, either from conviction or to attract donations, Khomeini was always neat and clean, saying that it was beneath the dignity of a cleric to look like a beggar. In his book *Khomeini: Life of the Ayatollah,* Baqer Moin explains Khomeini's unique approach to teaching.

> He also developed his own method of teaching. One of his students from this period, Ayatollah Ja'far Sobhani, who now lectures in Qom, recalls that instead of conducting his lectures as a dialectical argument between teacher and students, as was the custom, "He put forward a topic in a decisive manner, first explaining other opinions and then his own before looking for arguments. He never introduced issues that were unclear in his own mind, preferring to do his homework and reflect upon topics before discussing them." Khomeini was never particularly interested in discussion for its own sake, and he maintained this approach throughout his teaching career. The qualities of autocracy, decisiveness and self-righteousness that were to stand him in good stead in his later political career were already well ingrained in Khomeini, the young teacher.

circulates in my veins."[8] Khomeini led a protest movement among senior clerics that forced the shah to withdraw the bill. But in January 1963 the shah announced a new package of measures that included land reform (taking property from large landowners and dividing it among peasants) and women's suffrage. He called the reforms the White Revolution, to contrast them with a potential Communist or red revolution. The shah also wanted to give U.S. military personnel in Iran immunity from prosecution. Khomeini said that this would mean that American soldiers could beat, rape, or kill Iranians without fear of punishment.

Because of his outspoken opposition to this measure, Khomeini was arrested on June 5, 1963. Khomeini's supporters rioted in Qom by the thousands. The shah's troops killed at least twenty-eight demonstrators. Demonstrations also occurred in Tehran, Mashhad, Esfahan, and Shiraz. Hundreds—some observers estimated thousands—were killed when security forces opened fire on the crowds.

Many clerics expressed support for Khomeini and their opposition to the shah. In response, the shah launched a campaign claiming that Khomeini was acting on behalf of foreign nations. This was unsuccessful, however, and by early July the government released Khomeini from prison. He was soon placed under house arrest, however, and then in November 1964 Khomeini was exiled to Turkey. He later went to the city of Najaf in Iraq, where he stayed until 1978. During his exile, however, Khomeini kept in touch with his fellow opposition leaders in Iran, and his sermons were secretly distributed all over the country. This allowed Khomeini to respond effectively to the shah's policies. For exam-

Ayatollah Ruhollah Khomeini was the leader of the 1979 Islamic Revolution that changed the face of modern Iran.

ple, in March 1975 the shah established a new political party, the Rastakhiz (Resurgence) Party, and required all adults to join. This demand was seen as a threat because in the past the government had only required that opposition to its policies not be public. Now, however, failure to join the Rastakhiz could result in banishment, and failure to be an enthusiastic member might result in losing one's job. At about the same time, the shah switched the country from the Islamic lunar calendar to a solar "imperial" calendar. With this move, the Islamic calendar and its central role in the lives of Iranian Muslims was insulted. According to Moin,

From his place of exile in Najaf Khomeini responded to the advent of Rastakhiz [Party] with a long fatwa [Islamic legal judgment]. The creation of the party, he said, was the Shah's admission of the failure of his "White Revolution" or, as Khomeini put it, "his damned black revolution" . . . and to join it was forbidden. He produced another follow up statement three months later . . . in which he forbade the faithful from using the "imperial" calendar.[9]

The government could no longer punish Khomeini directly because he was out of the country, so it attempted to silence his followers and supporters in Iran. According to Moin,

Surveillance, arrest, torture and imprisonment were widely practised with the clergy . . . who maintained their contacts with Khomeini, collected and helped transmit funds to him, and from time to time used the pulpit to attack state policy. Ali Khamene'i, Mahdavi Kani, Musavi Ardebili, Montazeri, and Hashemi Rafsanjani [prominent leaders of the revolution] were all sentenced to spells of imprisonment or internal exile in the early 1970s.[10]

Some of those sent to prison died there, and allegations surfaced that their deaths were the result of torture.

The shah's harsh treatment of his opponents only led to more protests. In June 1975, on the twelfth anniversary of Khomeini's arrest, protesters staged a major demonstration in Qom that the authorities could not control. Government forces killed an estimated forty-five protesters and arrested three hundred. Galvanized by the government's actions, opposition forces began to unite, with dissident groups coordinating their activities for the first time. For example, in Tehran in 1977, eight committees began to organize public debates and protest demonstrations, pass out leaflets, enlist young people, and pass on Ayatollah Khomeini's instructions to key supporters.

Iran and the United States

Opponents of the shah hoped that foreign pressure on the shah to ease his repressive policies would increase when Jimmy Carter took office as president of the United States in January 1977. During his campaign for office Carter had emphasized the need to improve human rights around the world. Khomeini thought that the new American president might do something about the Pahlavi regime and essentially issued a challenge to Carter. At the time Khomeini said:

> We are now waiting to see whether the present American government is sacrificing its honour and that of the American people . . . to material interest in exploiting Iran, or by taking its support away from these dirty elements [the Pahlavi regime] to regain honour and integrity for its government.[11]

However, when the shah visited the United States in November 1977, neither he nor Carter announced any reforms. Moreover, the repression of dissent within Iran continued. For example, the Iranian secret police, SAVAK, violently broke up a protest meeting in Tehran on November 22, which resulted in many injuries and arrests.

Opposition leaders were further disheartened during a visit Carter made to Tehran in late December. At a state dinner on December 31, the president toasted the shah with champagne, declaring his friendship for the shah and speaking of the "respect, admiration and love of your people for you."[12] Carter's words ignored the obvious signs of public discontent with the shah, and the toast was also offensive to Khomeini and his followers because Islam forbids the drinking of alcohol. Then on January 6, 1978, the government-controlled press published an article sharply critical of Khomeini and even insulting him personally. This was seen by many Iranians as a serious breach of courtesy that signaled a lack of respect for Islam itself. The article set off several demonstrations, during which six protesters were killed. These deaths began a cycle of protests because in Islamic tradition, deaths are commemorated with prayers on

Muhammad Reza Shah Pahlavi (left) meets with President Jimmy Carter in Washington, D.C., to discuss the state of affairs in Iran.

the seventh and fortieth days after they occur. Opposition organizers were able to call out large crowds of protesters on the commemorative days, and these demonstrations resulted in further violent repression and more deaths. Due to the worsening situation, Khomeini finally declared publicly that the shah must be overthrown.

Paris

The Iranian government wanted Khomeini to be further isolated from his supporters in Iran, so in early October 1978 it pressured Iraq to expel the ayatollah. Khomeini tried to go to Kuwait but was refused entry, so he went instead to France, arriving on October 12. In Paris, Khomeini was among other Iranian exiles and had ample opportunities to publicize his views. Still, he was vague about his plans for a government to succeed the shah's regime. According to Moin,

> While emphasising the principles of Islam, Khomeini at this point spoke of a "progressive Islam" in which even a woman could become president and in which "Islamic rules of retribution would not be applied unless sufficient preparations had been made to implement Islamic justice in its totality." He . . . was careful to sidestep in public the issue of the nature of an Islamic state. He confined his statements on the Islamic content of the future political system of Iran to the need for the clergy to play a supervisory role—which was interpreted by most people to mean the position that clergy were supposed to exercise under the 1906 constitution. [13]

Khomeini's vagueness in Paris about his intentions was designed to help him hold together a diverse coalition of the shah's opponents, many of whom objected strongly to the idea of the Muslim clergy having a leading role in government. Nevertheless, the time for Khomeini to turn his theories into reality soon arrived. In 1978 the Ashura holiday, which commemorates the martyrdom of Imam Hussein in 680, fell on December 10 and 11.

As many as 17 million peaceful marchers, 2 to 3 million of them in Tehran, protested against the shah. It was clear that the end of the Pahlavi dynasty was approaching. Khomeini began making plans for a transitional government. When Muhammad Reza Shah Pahlavi left Tehran on January 16, 1979, the twenty-five-hundred-year-old tradition of dynastic rule in Iran came to an end.

The Islamic Republic of Iran

2

The revolution that swept Iran in 1978 and forced the abdication of the shah in January 1979 included many groups dissatisfied with the Pahlavi government, among them Muslim clerics, students, intellectuals, merchants, and women. Most regarded themselves as Shia Muslims, but they agreed on very little except that the shah had to go. Because of their wide differences in opinion, as soon as they forced the shah to leave the country, a battle for control of the new government began within the revolutionary coalition—a battle that has continued into the twenty-first century. At its core was the rivalry among three broad categories of people: conservative Muslim clerics; moderate Muslims, both clergy and laypeople; and secularists who wanted the clergy to have little or no role in government.

Cry It from the Rooftops

As the immediate success of the revolution became assured, most Iranians felt that their nation was entering a new and better chapter of its history. They were euphoric that the shah was gone and that Ayatollah Khomeini was returning, and they became increasingly bold and public in expressing their emotions. One peculiarly Iranian way this happened occurred at night. In Tehran, as in other Iranian cities, most houses have rooftop terraces that are used as evening gathering places and even as bedrooms in hot weather. Ana M. Briongos, a writer who has studied and traveled extensively in Iran, explains that

> The terraces of Tehran make up a vast discontinuous surface, on which, at the beginning of the Revolution, the inhabitants of the city gathered as night fell to chant in unison *Allaho Ak-*

bar, God is Great. The chanting spread throughout the city from terrace to terrace until the millions of voices joining together in the darkness sounded like an overwhelming roar coming directly from somewhere deep in the earth's core. Everyone who hoped that the return of Khomeini would gather the country's forces to bring about a necessary revolution went up onto the terraces. [14]

Their wish was granted—Khomeini was soon at the head of the new Islamic Republic of Iran, and he would remain the focal point of the nation until his death in 1989.

Khomeini was a conservative cleric whose views on government and society were rooted in Iranian Shia Islam as it was taught and practiced in the early twentieth century. Born in 1900, he had lived through several Iranian governments—the last two Qajar shahs, the chaotic Constitutional era, the two Pahlavi shahs, and the short-lived government of Prime Minister Muhammad Mosaddeq. Khomeini believed that all of these governments had failed for one reason: because they had failed to follow the principles of Islam.

The rooftop of a typical house in Iran. During the Islamic Revolution people gathered on rooftop terraces to pray for Khomeini's return.

Khomeini's Plan

Khomeini had published his views on the nature of Islamic government ten years before the revolution in two works, *Hukumat-i Islami* (Islamic Government) and *Jihad-i Akbar* (The Supreme Struggle). *Jihad-i Akbar* refers to Muhammad's saying that the supreme struggle is with the self and its tendency to rebel against God. In the orthodox Shii view, only Muhammad, his daughter Fatimah, and the twelve imams, or successors of Muhammad, had been completely successful in the supreme struggle. Khomeini, however, argued that through resolute faith and action a modern Muslim could achieve a similar status and thus, as the imams had been, become qualified to rule the people. This idea was a change from mainstream Shii thinking, in which religious scholars as a group served as advisers to the government. It was important for Iran because it laid the foundation for Khomeini's own later assumption of both the title of imam and the lifetime role of Supreme Leader of Iran.

In *Hukumat-i Islami,* Khomeini presented his thoughts on three aspects of bringing about an Islamic government: why Islamic government is necessary, what form it should take, and preliminary plans for implementing such a government. His belief was that the leader of the country should be an experienced, mature cleric (known as the *faqih*) who had earned the respect and trust of his colleagues and the people. Khomeini was convinced that a just society could only be achieved by having a senior Muslim cleric in ultimate charge of the nation because the clerics had devoted their lives to the study of *shariah,* or Islamic law, and so would be able to interpret it correctly. He felt that the *faqih* would resist any temptation to become a dictator or tyrant because he would not be motivated by personal gain and so would act in accordance with *shariah.*

While Khomeini viewed *shariah* as in some ways like the constitutions of Western countries, he thought *shariah* was vastly superior because it came from God. Thus Khomeini did not believe in Western-style democracy in which elected representatives make laws. Instead, he thought that God had already provided the

"A Government of Divine Justice"

While in exile, Ayatollah Khomeini led the revolution through his writings and speeches, which were recorded and distributed in Iran on cassette tapes. The following is Khomeini's message for Id al-Fitr, September 6, 1978, the holiday that ends the month-long Ramadan fast. During Ramadan that year—the last Ramadan before the shah's abdication—many protests against the shah resulted in bloodshed. This statement from Khomeini, which is included in the book *Islam and Revolution: Writings and Declarations of Imam Khomeini, 1941–1980,* translated by Hamid Algar, contributed to further protests the following two days, leading the shah's government to declare martial law on September 8, when an estimated half-million protesters took to the streets of Tehran.

> This year's 'Id al-Fitr has been an epic celebration of heroism for all segments of our population. It was a day that demonstrated to the whole world the intellectual and practical maturity of our people, and declared with the utmost clarity that the wish of the entire nation is for the Shah to leave, and for his regime of oppression and exploitation of our Muslim people to be abolished. After performing the 'Id prayer, the Muslim people of Iran performed another valuable act of worship by uttering thundering cries of protest against this tyrannical bandit regime and demanding a government of divine justice. To struggle for the sake of these goals is one of the greatest forms of worship, and to make sacrifices for them is in conformity with the customs of the prophets, particularly the Most Noble Messenger of Islam [Muhammad] and his great successor, the Commander of the Faithful [the first imam, Ali ibn Abi Talib].

basic laws that society needed and that God would guide the *faqih* in the administration of the government. Khomeini also wrote that while the *faqih*'s ultimate authority came from God, he should govern with the advice of other clerics and with an elected consultative assembly known as the Majlis. His view at this time— ten years before the revolution—was that the role of the *faqih* was to set out principles and settle disputes, not to be a day-to-day manager of the government.

Not surprisingly, the idea of the *faqih* as a detached and contemplative leader whose primary task was determining the will of God for his country matched Khomeini's own style perfectly. It is unclear, however, whether he fully appreciated the range and depth of problems that would face the Islamic Republic. Moin writes that Khomeini's

> worldview was set to the reincarnation of a society that has not been in existence since the death of the Prophet in the seventh century. A skilled practitioner of clerical politics, a master tactician who succeeded in bringing disparate opposition groups together, and a supreme strategist of revolution, Khomeini's only goal was the recreation of an idealized past. But those in Iran who awaited his return were looking above all for a better future—and not necessarily only in spiritual terms. [15]

Khomeini's attempt to translate his vision into government policies and institutions soon produced a range of problems. Because of the ambiguity inherent in Khomeini's role—he had wide-ranging powers but often delegated them, and he could interfere in matters not reserved to him—a vast field was left open within the Shii community for disputes to arise among people with competing interests. This was even more the case with the Western-educated intellectuals and others who were more interested in a secular, democratic government than a cleric-dominated Islamic Republic. During 1979, struggles for power broke out at all levels, and Iran once again found itself in chaos.

The Early Days of the Islamic Republic

The coalition that had worked to bring down the shah began to dissolve even before Khomeini left the airplane that brought him back to Tehran. The revolutionary mullahs boarded the plane first and told anyone they did not consider sufficiently orthodox to leave the plane so that they would not be photographed with Khomeini. Even old friends who had been with Khomeini in

Paris were excluded. In his memoir of the revolutionary era, Abol Hassan Bani-Sadr, a close adviser who later became president of Iran, said, "It seemed that the duty of the intellectuals was to bring Khomeini to Tehran and hand him over to the mollahs."[16]

But for both the religious and secular leaders of the revolution, one of their chief goals was removing Western—especially American and British—influence from Iran's oil industry. Just as Prime Minister Muhammad Mosaddeq had done in 1953, in February 1979 the new Islamic government nationalized the oil industry. Nationalization would allow Iran to keep all the revenue from oil sales instead of splitting it with the foreign companies. However, after the 1953 nationalization, the U.S. Central Intelligence Agency engineered Mosaddeq's removal as prime minister and a return to foreign control of Iran's oil, and so many Iranians feared that the United States would again intervene and return the shah to power. Their fears were heightened when U.S. president Jimmy Carter granted the shah entry to the United States for medical treatment in October 1979.

The Hostage Crisis

Khomeini's government demanded the shah's return to Iran to face trial, but the United States refused to turn over its former ally. On November 4, 1979, a small group of Iranian students took matters into their own hands. They seized the U.S. embassy in Tehran and took sixty-six diplomats and staff hostage. Although fourteen hostages were soon released, the students held the remaining fifty-two. Their main demand was that the United States return the shah to Iran. At first Khomeini wanted the students to leave the embassy, but it soon became clear that the people of Iran overwhelmingly supported the students. On November 7, Khomeini announced that it would be possible to negotiate the release of the hostages only if "the U.S. extradites the deposed shah, the top enemy of our dear nation Iran, and refrains from espionage against our movement."[17]

In response to the hostage crisis, the United States stopped imports of Iranian oil, denied the Iranian government access to its

*Angered over U.S. support for the shah, protesters burn an
American flag atop the U.S. embassy in Tehran.*

bank accounts in the United States, refused to ship spare parts for
military equipment, and imposed an economic blockade. But the
students and the Muslim clerics who backed them were unwill-
ing to compromise, and the more moderate members of the government found themselves powerless to intervene. The new
president, Abol Hassan Bani-Sadr, opposed holding the hostages,
but Khomeini overruled him. Encouraged by demonstrations in
other countries in support of the embassy seizure, Khomeini was
confident that the United States would eventually grant Iran important concessions.

The Bani-Sadr Presidency

President Bani-Sadr faced a wide range of problems in addition to
his disagreement with Khomeini over the hostages. An Islamic in-
tellectual who before the revolution had enjoyed a close relationship with Khomeini, Bani-Sadr was elected president in January
1980 with a 75 percent majority. The support of the electorate did
not insulate him from infighting among the leaders of Iran, though,
and Bani-Sadr soon discovered that Khomeini not only disagreed

with him on policy matters but in some ways also actively opposed him.

Bani-Sadr had little power and few resources to tackle Iran's many difficulties. In a very short time Iran had gone from being a friend of the powerful Western nations to being almost totally isolated. The hostage crisis got the lion's share of press attention, but many other issues contributed to an image of Iran as a nation that was too unstable to be trusted, among them the nationalization of the oil industry; the wholesale execution of former members of the shah's government; insurgencies among Iran's Turkoman, Kurdish, and Arabic minorities; and armed vigilante groups known as *hezbollahis* enforcing revolutionary correctness.

Internally, Iran's government was virtually paralyzed. At first Khomeini seemed to give his old friend Bani-Sadr strong support by allowing him to be sworn in before the Majlis session began, giving him command of the armed forces, and naming him head of the Revolutionary Council, Khomeini's handpicked committee of advisers. But Khomeini soon began to undermine the president. For example, Khomeini often appointed people to important posts without consulting Bani-Sadr, and he failed to support those Bani-Sadr appointed to other jobs. Bani-Sadr faced strong opposition from other quarters. A chief thorn in his side was the Islamic Republican Party (IRP), which represented the views and interests of clerics sympathetic to Khomeini, and they often acted to sabotage Bani-Sadr's administration. Their goal was to have as much power as possible in the hands of the clerics.

The perception that Bani-Sadr had little control over the government was reinforced in May 1979 when Khomeini authorized the formation of the Pasdaran-e Enghelab-e Islami (Islamic Revolutionary Guards). They were to serve as bodyguards for clerics who were the targets of Communist terrorists as well as a military force that could help to control civil unrest and eventually counterbalance (and perhaps replace) the regular army. Bani-Sadr wanted to disband the Revolutionary Guards, but the IRP's leaders objected, and their view prevailed over the president's. Bani-Sadr was not even able to select his own prime minister, being forced to accept the IRP nominee, Muhammad Ali Rajai. Bani-Sadr's disputes with others in the government and the revolutionary movement only escalated. He was forced from office in June 1981 and later went into exile in France.

The Khamenei Administration

The prime minister with whom Bani-Sadr had had so many conflicts, Muhammad Ali Rajai, was elected to succeed him as president. But Rajai himself became a victim of the turmoil and violence that had gripped the country, being assassinated shortly after his election. Another election was held in October 1981, and a mid-ranking cleric, Hojjatoeslam Seyed Ali Khamenei, was elected. (Khamenei was destined to be a dominant figure in Iranian politics for many years to come—when Ayatollah Khomeini died in 1989, Khamenei was selected as Supreme Leader.)

The early years of Khamenei's presidency were marked by a virtual civil war between the clerical faction, of which he was a leader, and a variety of groups that objected to clerics having command of the government. Khamenei maintained control, however,

Tehran residents and Islamic Republican soldiers show support for Ayatollah Khomeini during the Islamic Revolution.

through superior force on the streets and the execution of literally thousands of political opponents. Under Khamenei the institutions of government, most of which had been created in the months following the fall of the Pahlavi dynasty, were still largely ineffective in dealing with the nation's ills.

In addition to the daunting domestic problems Khamenei and his administration faced, they also fought an eight-year war with the neighboring country of Iraq. Khamenei chaired the Supreme Defense Council during the war, overseeing the conduct of one of the longest and bloodiest conflicts of the twentieth century.

Iran at War

Relations between Iran and Iraq had not been friendly for many years, mainly because of a dispute over control of the Shatt al Arab waterway, which is Iraq's only access to the Persian Gulf. The two countries had reached an agreement over use of the waterway in 1975, but in 1979 both countries had a change in government. At about the same time that Ayatollah Khomeini assumed control of Iran, Saddam Hussein came to power in Iraq. Saddam wanted full ownership of the Shatt al Arab for Iraq, and he also wanted to prevent Iran from inciting rebellion in Iraq, which has a 60-percent Shii majority population. The Iraqi leader had good reason to be fearful—Ayatollah Khomeini had publicly called for the Shia of Iraq to rise up against Saddam, whose secularist government Khomeini considered un-Islamic.

In September 1980, Saddam Hussein launched a surprise attack on Iran. Saddam thought that the Iranians would be easy to defeat because Iran was in the midst of civil chaos and the Iranian military had been weakened by purges of officers who had served under the shah and by the U.S. cutoff of shipments of spare parts for weapons. But to the surprise of many, the attack pulled the Iranian people together, and thousands volunteered to join the army. With few resources to provide training, weapons, or equipment, and brutal trench-warfare conditions at the front, Iranian soldiers experienced terrible hardships and a catastrophic casualty rate. The battles along the border raged on, with Iraq taking territory and then losing it in a seemingly endless cycle.

Tens of thousands of teenage Iranians volunteered to serve their country in the war against Iraq.

Though he did not achieve the quick victory he at first anticipated, Saddam thought that the Iranians would soon give up the fight, that their sacrifices to continue the war would be too great for them to bear. He was wrong. During the war, journalists John Simpson and Tira Shubart visited the battle lines and found that Iran's soldiers were committed to the war to a degree almost unheard of in other conflicts:

> "Land is land—it doesn't matter. It's just earth and rock. We can give it back to the Iraqis after the war. What matters is the victory of Allah. This isn't a war for territory, it's a war for Allah."

The speaker was a short, intense young man in a ragged uniform, who was educated in the gentle city of Norwich, in England: about as far from this barren shell-blasted waste as it was possible to imagine. Around him, a crowd of twenty or thirty of his fellow volunteers were anxious to make sure the point was not lost on the questioner. "Allahu Akbar!" they chanted, having recognised the one word "Allah" in what he was saying. It was impossible for a foreign journalist to visit the war front without hearing this sort of thing; and it seemed to be entirely genuine.

Still it was hard for post-industrial, Western man to accept at face value. Who ordered them to say this kind of thing? Were they rewarded for saying it? How, after the enormous losses of so many years of fighting, could they maintain any form of enthusiasm for it? The obvious comparison for Europeans is with the First World War: the mud, the shelling, the trench fighting, the use of gas, the huge offensives bogging down after gaining a few hundred yards—it all has a familiar ring. But the First World War lasted for four years, and by 1917 the morale of each of the main armies was stretched almost to breaking point. By contrast, the Iran-Iraq war began in September 1980 and continued until July 1988. There were no reports of serious mutinies on the Iranian side, no evidence that the men were turning on their officers or surrendering voluntarily, no suggestion of any of the other symptoms of war-weariness. [18]

The 1989 Constitutional Revision

After eight years of bloodshed, the war ended in a stalemate. The Islamic Republic had achieved a form of success in its first ten years—it had not been defeated by Iraq, and Ayatollah Khomeini had not been overthrown. Nevertheless, the government was weak and often ineffective, due in part to the inconsistencies and contradictions in Khomeini's policies. He hoped his charisma would motivate the people to build a new Iran, but he realized that he would soon die and that no one could fully replace him. Khomeini wanted Iran to be guided by Islamic law, but he feared that having clerics in charge of the government would tempt them to abuse their power. Furthermore, Khomeini wanted Iran to be a just, prosperous, and smoothly functioning society that would be the envy of the entire world, but he distrusted the materialism, commercialism, and technology of the West that made prosperity and efficient government possible.

Because Ayatollah Khomeini knew that his charismatic style of leadership was partly to blame for the persistent economic and social problems, when a group of respected clerics and politicians proposed revising the constitution, Khomeini supported the effort. The 1979 constitution had been tailored to fit Khomeini, who was both the acknowledged religious leader of Iran (the *marja-e taqlid*) and its political leader (the *rahab*). Because no one else was likely to be able to fill both roles, the requirement that the Supreme Leader also be the *marja-e taqlid* was dropped. Under the new constitution, the Supreme Leader was to be chosen by the Assembly of Experts (an elected body of Islamic legal scholars) from among a number of clerics who had an understanding of Islamic law sufficient to guide the nation. In practice, the deciding factor in choosing the Supreme Leader would now be political skill.

The revision of the constitution that began shortly before Khomeini's death in June 1989 addressed another of the problems that had plagued the Islamic Republic during its first decade: the overlapping duties of the president and prime minister. This was solved by abolishing the office of prime minister, making the president more clearly in charge of the day-to-day operation of the government. The new constitution was ratified in a referendum on July 9, 1989.

Under the new constitution, most of the original government bodies were retained, but some were modified. For example, in both the 1979 and 1989 constitutions, the Assembly of Experts was empowered to select the Supreme Leader, review his performance and fitness for office, and can remove him if he becomes incapacitated or otherwise proves unable to perform his duties. The first assembly was composed of clerics and other leaders, but since then membership has been limited to clerics. Members are elected to eight-year terms, and they can hold other administrative jobs in the government or be members of the Majlis.

Disputes among the branches of government were a major destabilizing force during the first ten years of the Islamic Republic. In 1988, Khomeini established another group known as the Expediency Council, and it was retained in the 1989 constitution. The

Revolutionary Style

Though the veiling of women has gotten most of the media attention since the revolution, writer Ana M. Briongos, who studied and traveled in Iran before and after the revolution, says that men have also been affected. In her book *Black on Black: Iran Revisited,* she explains that before the revolution, men in Tehran dressed like their Western counterparts, in suits and ties, and they were clean shaven or wore mustaches. But when Briongos visited Tehran in the 1990s, that had changed.

Men in Tehran today look quite different from the way they looked during the time of the Shah. The tie and the clean-shaven face are signs of Western civilization, and as such have been banished. It is normal to have a couple of days' growth or a longer, well-groomed beard, a dark or grey suit, neither too new nor too well pressed, and for merchants in the bazaar, a waistcoat [vest] and a white shirt with an unstarched collar, or better still without a collar, and buttoned up to the neck. Shoes tend to be large, with uppers that can be squashed down at the heel so they can be worn like slippers. Iranian men never really took to the completely clean-shaven look, not even in the old days [before the revolution], and less still now. Before the Islamic Revolution, moustaches were standard: big handlebars, little Hitler-style stripes or the Stalin model. Now they all have undesirable connotations, though they're not absolutely forbidden of course. It's better to grow a beard if you're applying for a job, asking for a raise or negotiating a contract, just as Western men in such situations shave carefully, make sure their suit is well pressed and put on a tie.

Expediency Council advises the Supreme Leader on major policy decisions and resolves disputes among the executive, legislative, and judiciary branches of the government. In general, its decisions have favored the more conservative elements in the government.

Even though the 1989 constitution eliminated the office of prime minister, the president's powers are still limited, and he can accomplish very little without the support of the Majlis, the Guardian Council, the Expediency Council, and, ultimately, the Supreme Leader. The president is selected every four years through a national election and thus represents the interests of the voters; despite this, many presidential initiatives have been blocked by these other agencies.

The Voice of the People

The other popularly elected body in the Iranian government is the Majlis, the nation's legislature. Much of the political debate and dissent in the Islamic Republic has been expressed on the floor of the Majlis. Under the 1989 constitution, the Majlis has 290 members who serve four-year terms. Of these, 285 represent voting districts around the country with roughly equal population. For example, Tehran Province is divided into 38 districts. The remainder of the members represent the country's religious minorities.

Ayatollah Khomeini's version of democracy was limited to the election of a consultative assembly within a cleric-dominated government, and the constitutional revision did not change this. Though the Majlis would be the most effective voice of the people of Iran, its power was limited by the twelve-member Guardian Council. According to the NetIran website,

Motions and bills passed by the Majlis do not automatically become law. . . . The Guardian Council, as it is known for short, is in effect an upper house of parliament with the power to vote out the lower house's resolutions. It is assigned to check the laws passed by the Majlis, compare them with the provisions of the Islamic canon [legal principles] and the constitution, and ratify them, or return them to the House for being amended.[19]

In addition to having veto power over laws passed by the Majlis, the Guardian Council also was given the power to examine the credentials of potential election candidates. This gave the Guardian Council substantial control over who could be elected to the Majlis.

Despite the reforms contained in the 1989 constitution, Iran would continue to encounter many difficulties: inefficient and often ineffective government programs, conflicts between conservative clerics in high administrative and judicial posts and reform-minded elected officials, and poor relations with both neighboring Muslim countries and Western nations.

Chronic Instability

3

The decades before and after the founding of the Islamic Republic of Iran were characterized by constant change, and instability continues to be a major challenge for the nation. This is not surprising—the Iranians replaced a monarchy that had been in effect through various dynasties for over two thousand years. They had little experience with other forms of government, and the Islamic clerics who dominated the political landscape explicitly rejected Western models of democratic government and economic development, which they said would lead to moral decay. They were trying to devise a new system based on the theories of Shii Muslim governance advocated by Ayatollah Khomeini. As the Islamic Republic was born, Khomeini felt that Iran would at last experience the peace and international prestige he had envisioned for it during his long years of exile. But competing interests and personalities would soon overwhelm the nation and result in further bloodshed and unrest.

Changes in Education

One of the fundamental institutions of Iranian society—its education system—has proved to be a prime source of instability. Education in Iran has been used at various times either to promote or to exclude Western influences, and these sometimes rapid and drastic changes in curriculum were reflected in society at large. Western-style secular education in Iran began in the early nineteenth century when Iran's leaders decided to develop a European-trained army. First Iran sent cadets to European military schools, and then in 1851 it formed its own military academy staffed by instructors from Austria and Prussia. This experiment in Western education had some surprising results. According to historian Roy Mottahedeh, the Iranians learned more than just military skills from their European teachers:

They learned the nineteenth-century European ideologies of nationalism and progress. A "people" should unite themselves in one nation-state, whose government belonged to the people and expressed their common interests. This sense of common interest, and the sacrifices it demanded, could reach the masses only through education. [20]

As more Iranians were exposed to democracy through Western-style education, visits to Iran by Europeans, and Iranians traveling in Europe, pressure increased for Iran to adopt

Iranian boys study the Quran at an Islamic school. The mullahs banned Western-style education after the revolution.

a constitution that would limit the power of the shah and grant full civil rights to minorities. One Iranian leader of the time, Mostashar ad-Dowleh, wrote, "It is self-evident that in the future no nation—Islamic or non-Islamic—will continue to exist without constitutional law. . . . The various ethnic groups that live in Iran will not become one people until the law upholds their right to freedom of expression and the opportunity for education."[21] After many years of agitation and protest, in August 1906 the Qajar ruler Muzaffar ad-Din Shah agreed to the formation of an elective assembly and on December 30 of that year signed the new constitution it had drafted.

The trend toward Western, non-Islamic education continued. Under Reza Shah Pahlavi the trend even moved down to primary education as he attempted to transform Iran into a modern and secular state. According to Sandra Mackey,

> For a thousand years, elementary education resided in the *maktab,* the Koran school, where the pious, in exchange for the modest fees they collected from their students, taught the rudiments of reading, writing, and arithmetic in the context of religion. But religious education could claim no place in Reza Shah's Iran. To attain its nationalist goals, his new state required modern, technical education. As a result, Islamic schools, Christian missionary schools, and schools of the religious minorities closed their doors under Reza Shah's orders. All Iranians—male and female—went into free, compulsory education. By the end of Reza Shah's reign [1941], only one form of primary and secondary education remained. It was secular and it belonged to the state. Within it, students acquired knowledge of the glories of the vanished Persian Empire and learned to be loyal, patriotic citizens of the equally glorious Pahlavi state.[22]

Despite the efforts of the Pahlavis to suppress Islamic education and make it obsolete, the mullahs continued to teach the faithful. In 1978, it was the men of the *madrassahs,* the ancient system of Muslim colleges, who were at the center of the revolution. In the end, the *madrassah*-educated mullahs drove out the modernizers of education and returned Iran's educational system to an Islamic focus. They also sought to purge the nation of the effects of decades of Western-style education under the Pahlavi shahs.

Political Turmoil and Civil Strife

The new leaders of Iran shared a common religious background, but there were often intense conflicts between the *madrassah*-educated clerics and the nonclerics who had received more Western-style educations. The result was frequent changes in leadership. For example, Khomeini's choice for interim prime minister was Mehdi Bazargan, an Islamic socialist educated in the West. But Bazargan resigned two days after the start of the hostage crisis in November 1979 when it became clear that he had lost control of the government to the clerics.

Iran's first elected president, Abol Hassan Bani-Sadr, also fought constant political battles with the clerics. He eventually went underground in fear for his life in June 1981 after Khomeini had stripped him of his role as commander in chief of the military, the Majlis impeached him, and street mobs called for his death. Bani-Sadr later fled the country, making his way to France.

With Bani-Sadr's ouster, the conservative clerics controlled virtually all the important public institutions in Iran, but their hold on the people was more tenuous. Opposing the clerics were intellectuals, technical workers, and businesspeople who wanted Iran to continue on the path of modernization that had been started by the shah. Many of these people were Muslims who supported the idea of an Islamic republic as long as it included strong democratic institutions and a relatively free market. The most immediate and serious threat to the clerics, though, was posed by Islamic socialists, who wanted the government to combine Islamic principles with socialism and who objected to the clerics having a prominent role in governing. The most militant wing of the socialists was the Mujahedin-e Khalq, which had a guerrilla army of

Xerxes and Persian Kingship

One of the emperors of the early Persian Empire was Xerxes, who ruled from 486 to 465 B.C. Early in his reign he directed that an inscription be made describing his kingship. It contains many of the elements that have characterized Persia and Iran in the twenty-five hundred years since then: worship of and dependence on God; rule based on divine favor and in pursuit of justice; and the encouragement of good and prevention of evil, especially the evil of worshiping multiple gods. Because all of these ideas were present in Ayatollah Khomeini's teachings as well, many in Iran hoped that the Islamic Revolution would be a return to some of the ancient principles of Iranian government. Historian A.T. Olmstead records the inscription in his book *History of the Persian Empire*.

> A great god is Ahuramazda, who created this earth, who created man, who created peace for man, who made Xerxes king, one king of many, lord of many.
>
> I am Xerxes, the great king, king of kings, king of lands containing many men, king of this great earth far and wide, son of Darius the king, an Achaemenid, a Persian, son of a Persian, an Aryan, of Aryan seed. . . .
>
> Says Xerxes the king: When I became king, there was within these lands . . . one which was restless [the province of Bactria]. Afterward Ahuramazda [God] brought me help. By the favor of Ahuramazda I smote that land and put it in its place. . . .
>
> [W]ithin these lands was a place where formerly the daevas [lesser gods] were worshiped. Afterward by the favor of Ahuramazda I destroyed that community . . . and proclaimed: the daevas you shall not worship. Where formerly the daevas were worshiped, there I worshiped Ahuramazda and the holy Arta [righteousness].
>
> And there was other business which was done ill; that I made good. That which I did, all I did by the favor of Ahuramazda. Ahuramazda brought me aid until I had finished the work.

perhaps a hundred thousand and several times that many supporters overall. According to Mackey,

> Although . . . the clerics controlled the executive, legisla-
> tive, and judicial institutions of state, ran the National Iran-
> ian Oil Company, possessed the Revolutionary Guards as
> the parallel of the army, and dispensed patronage simulta-
> neously from government coffers and organizations of the
> revolution, they could not deliver stability. Chaos swirled
> out of personal rivalries and old grudges. Turmoil en-
> veloped the technocrats and professionals desperately
> needed to develop the country, sending them fleeing in
> fear and frustration. Anarchy made itself felt in the griev-
> ances that ethnic groups and tribes hurled against a disin-
> tegrating central government. . . . One more phase of the
> revolution had yet to be fought. It would pit the political
> clerics against the Islamic Left, represented primarily by
> the Mujahedin-e Khalq. [23]

The Mujahedin-e Khalq had once been aligned with the clerics in that they had both opposed the Pahlavi regime. The clerics had mainly used protests and their religious authority to fight
the shah, but the Mujahedin had used guerrilla warfare tactics
against the shah's military and secret police beginning in the
early 1970s. In the early 1980s they had a large core of experienced fighters when their new battle with Khomeini's government began. The flashpoint was Khomeini's refusal to allow the
Mujahedin's leader to run for president, which led the Mujahedin to support President Bani-Sadr in his opposition to
Khomeini's policies.

But the Mujahedin's support of Bani-Sadr was not enough to
keep him in the presidency. After his removal from office in June
1981, the Mujahedin felt stymied in their attempts to influence policy through political means. Within a few days they began a pro-
gram of terror attacks against the Islamic Republican Party, the
ruling clerical party. The first casualty was Khomeini's protégé, Ali
Khamenei, who was injured when a bomb hidden in a tape recorder

exploded during his Friday sermon. The next day, seventy-four leaders of the IRP were killed when a trash can filled with explosives was detonated during a meeting. Among the dead was a key Khomeini adviser, Ayatollah Muhammad Beheshti, who headed both the IRP and Iran's judiciary.

Though the regime responded with massive arrests and executions, the Mujahedin's campaign continued. In the elections of July 1981, from which the Mujahedin candidate had been excluded, Muhammad Ali Rajai won the presidency and Muhammad Javad Bahonar was selected as prime minister. The following month, Rajai, Bahonar, and ten other leaders met to discuss ways to curb the Mujahedin's attacks, which by then had claimed the lives of over two hundred government officials. During their talks a bomb hidden in the wall of the meeting room exploded, killing six, including Rajai and Bahonar.

The Khomeini regime used every means at its disposal to stop the terror campaign, such as recruiting and arming mullahs and teaming them with units of the Revolutionary Guards. The result, according to Sandra Mackey, was a reign of counterterror:

> Turned loose with unrestricted power, they [the Revolutionary Guards] ruthlessly suppressed street demonstrations, entered homes at will, made unauthorized arrests, and fed the machine of execution. By September, fifty people a day routinely went before the firing squad or were hanged from scaffolding, bridges, and on one occasion, the crossbar of a swing set on a children's playground. Too often, courts in search of blood randomly chose their victims. Royalists already in jail, the despised Bahais [a non-Islamic religious group], and a twelve-year-old accused of participating in a demonstration, all went to their deaths. [24]

The war between the clerics and the socialists caused thousands of casualties and continued until late in 1982. By then many of the Mujahedin had been killed, had gone into hiding, or had fled Iran. Ayatollah Khomeini, in a bid to restore some measure of peace and security to his country, issued a declaration aimed at

Ayatollah Khamenei

Iran's Supreme Leader, Ayatollah Seyed Ali Khamenei, was born in 1939 in Mashhad in Khorasan Province. Khamenei began his study of theology there under Haj Sheikh Hashem Qazvini and Ayatollah Milani, followed by a brief stay in Najaf in 1957. He moved to Qom in 1958 to study under Ayatollahs Borujerdi and Khomeini, returning to Mashhad in 1963. Like Khomeini, Khamenei was a critic of Shah Muhammad Reza Pahlavi, and he was frequently harassed by the shah's secret intelligence agency, SAVAK. After his first arrest in 1963 he began to conduct his classes in Mashhad in secret. He was arrested several times and spent a year in prison in the mid-1970s for his antigovernment activities. He lost the use of his right arm when he was injured in a bomb attack by political rivals in 1981, shortly after the revolution. Khamenei served as Iran's president from 1981 to 1989. He became Supreme Leader after the death of Ayatollah Khomeini in 1989.

Volunteer forces salute Ayatollah Khamenei. Khamenei has served as Iran's president and Supreme Leader.

stopping abuses of power by the Revolutionary Guards and the judiciary, and guaranteeing minimal civil rights.

Ethnic Conflicts and the Iran-Iraq War

The turmoil in the streets coincided with renewed demands from Iran's ethnic minorities, who lived mainly in Iran's border provinces, for a larger role in the new republic. For centuries, ethnic conflicts had plagued Iran, compounded as they were with religious differences. This was especially true in the early days of the Islamic Republic. The power vacuum created by the dissolution of the Pahlavi regime occasioned the airing of long-held grievances by three ethnic minorities: the Turkomans, the Khuzistan Arabs, and the Kurds.

The Turkoman minority in Gorgan, 150 miles northeast of Tehran, demanded land reform—more control over their ancestral territories—but their movement was put down by force. In Khuzistan, an oil-producing region at the northern end of the Persian Gulf, ethnic Arabs wanted a larger share of oil revenues, jobs, and more official recognition of Arabic language and culture. The Tehran government thought that the protests and subsequent demonstrations were inspired by Iraqi agents. Several demonstrators died when troops fired on them. After the demonstrations, their leader was sent to Qom and kept under house arrest, and the movement died out.

The problem of the Kurds was more difficult to resolve. They wanted to change the borders of the province of Kurdistan to take in more of the Kurdish-speaking population of Iran, and they wanted a larger share of tax money to be spent on their needs, recognition of Kurdish as an official language, and local autonomy. When negotiations between Kurdish leaders and the Tehran government broke down in August 1979, fighting resulted. Khomeini sent in the Iranian army to quell the uprising.

The problems caused by these ethnic conflicts were dwarfed by the effects on Iran of its war with Iraq. Hundreds of thousands of Iranians were left homeless. Iran's lack of military supplies meant that its soldiers were often outgunned. The official Iranian policy was to use human-wave tactics to fight the Iraqis, send-

Kurdish soldiers in 1970. The Kurds are one of several main ethnic minorities that live in Iran.

ing thousands of soldiers to face withering artillery, machine-gun fire, and even poison gas. The Iranians used a variant of this tactic recruiting teenagers and old men to perform virtual suicide missions, such as running ahead of Iranian soldiers to detonate mines laid by Iraqi defenders. Their losses were staggering, with perhaps two hundred thousand Iranians killed and a million wounded.

The war weakened the economy by interfering with oil exports and turning workers into soldiers, increased the national debt, worsened relations with Iran's neighbors and Western nations, decimated a generation of young people, and produced

Muhammad Khatami

Like the Ayatollahs Khomeini and Khamenei, Iran's current president Muhammad Khatami also studied at a seminary in the Iranian religious center of Qom. He earned the rank of *hojjatoeslam,* a mid-level cleric. His father was a respected religious leader in Iran and a friend of Khomeini.

Born in Yazd in 1943, Khatami became involved in Khomeini's opposition movement in the 1960s, printing and distributing leaflets and organizing debates. In 1978 Khatami was sent to Hamburg, Germany, to establish an Islamic center there, but he returned to Iran after the revolution to serve in the Majlis, Iran's parliament.

Appointed minister of Culture and Islamic Guidance in 1982, Khatami began to ease some of the restrictions that had been placed on literature, music, art, and film by conservative Islamic legislators after the revolution. Conservatives disapproved of Khatami's relatively liberal policies, which included allowing a female pop singer to hold a concert in Tehran, albeit for a female audience, in 1992. Following the concert, Khatami was forced to resign. He then became head of the National Library in Tehran and cultural adviser to then-president Ali Akbar Hashemi Rafsanjani. When Rafsanjani's second term ended, Khatami ran for president in 1997 and won by a landslide. Reelected by another landslide in 2001, Khatami has continued to push for reform in Iran.

Students at Tehran University show their support for President Muhammad Khatami.

another generation heavily weighted with orphans. Over a decade after the war's end, Iran was still experiencing its destabilizing effects.

A Weak Democracy

Like so many other aspects of Iranian society, the nation's approach to democracy is fraught with contradictions. As in other countries, elections and referenda have been used to give legitimacy to Iran's constitutions and the nation's leaders, but at times the Islamic Republic has used elections in ways that some Western observers believe have contributed to instability and conflict. The first example of this was the referendum held at the end of March 1979 to determine the type of government the country would have. Many prominent Iranians who had participated in the overthrow of the shah wanted Islam to have a limited role in government. Despite their protests, Ayatollah Khomeini insisted that the only form of government that would appear on the ballot was an Islamic republic and that the voting would not be secret. Critics said that these factors, and the lack of clarity about just what shape the republic would take, led to the 98 percent vote in favor.

The story of the adoption of Iran's constitution illustrates how the competing factions in Iranian politics sowed the seeds of future instability. Interim prime minister Mehdi Bazargan's government prepared the first draft of the constitution, which was finished in June 1979. It was essentially a revision of the 1906 constitution, substituting a strong presidency for the monarchy. The clergy were not given a prominent role, and the office of Supreme Leader was not even mentioned. Oddly, Khomeini at first wanted to submit this draft to a referendum as soon as possible, but there were protests from several political groups, especially liberal Islamists and socialists, who hoped to have provisions written into the constitution that would be favorable to their interests. Khomeini relented and agreed to submit the draft constitution to the Assembly of Experts for revision before it was submitted to a vote.

But the Assembly of Experts was dominated by conservative clerics, and the constitution it drafted between August and

November 1979 was even less to the liking of the groups that had protested against the first draft. The revised constitution established the Supreme Leader as the final authority in Iran and gave broad powers to clergy in the judiciary and allowed clergy to hold other posts as well, such as in the Majlis. Thus, the original protests by those who wanted to exclude clerics from government actually resulted in the exact opposite—a government in which most of the power and authority was vested in the Supreme Leader and other members of the clergy.

The 1979 constitution resulted in a government that was often at odds with itself and unable to take effective action to solve the nation's problems. Though the 1989 revisions to the constitution eliminated the office of prime minister and seemed to give more power to the popularly elected president, it did nothing to lessen the potential for conflict between the president and the other centers of power in the government—the Supreme Leader, the Majlis, the Guardian Council, and the Assembly of Experts.

Rafsanjani and Reform

The first president elected under the 1989 constitution, Ali Akbar Hashemi Rafsanjani, for a while looked as though he would be able to bridge the differences between the conservative clerics and the reformers. Though Rafsanjani was himself a cleric, he was concerned about the practicalities of daily life as well as spiritual matters. Among his goals were increasing employment, providing more and better housing, building and staffing schools, and providing medical services. But his attempts at change sometimes backfired. He tried to remove from government, especially from the Majlis, the hard-liners who had shaped many government decisions and had made diplomatic relations with the West more difficult. But in the 1992 elections, the Majlis members who replaced those ousted by Rafsanjani were also conservative and refused to pass many of the reform measures proposed by him. Reform efforts stalled, and the Iranian public began to wonder whether their lives would ever improve.

In Rafsanjani's second term, from 1993 to 1997, his relationship soured with the Supreme Leader, Ayatollah Khamenei, and he was unable to persuade the Majlis to support his programs. Enforcement of restrictions on public behavior increased, and even private activities such as watching videotapes or programs from satellite television were targeted for prosecution, leading to many arrests and heightening fear among ordinary Iranians of a return to a police state. The unstable relationships among the Islamic Republic's branches of government had again—and not for the last time—initiated a round of internal political conflicts that caused many observers to wonder whether Iran was in transition toward the more democratic society reformers called for or toward new forms of political and cultural repression.

A Society in Conflict 4

Few nations have been as much defined by their internal conflicts as Iran. The nation's conflicts at the beginning of the twenty-first century were similar to those of earlier times: disputes over the role of women in society, the right to free speech and free press, the role of business and entrepreneurship in an Islamic society, the role of the clergy in government and daily life, and how the government should govern, for example, how order should be maintained and crime prosecuted.

Chadors and Bikinis

Ever since the attempts of the first Pahlavi shah in the 1930s to modernize Iran, the most visible gauge of cultural conflict in Iran has been clothing, especially for women. When journalist Robin Wright first visited Iran as a young reporter in 1973, Americans and Western ways were welcome there. Iran during the 1970s was "an openly inviting place for an American woman. I felt as relaxed about traveling throughout the country as I did in Europe. I could go most places, do virtually anything, talk to anyone and dress in whatever apparel I chose. Short skirts were acceptable. After all, Iranians wore bikinis on the beach."[25] But after the revolution, women were required to wear *hejab,* a general term for modest dress. Many adopted the chador, a one-piece wrap that covers the entire body except the hands and face. Some Iranian women who preferred the Western clothing styles encouraged under the Pahlavi regime—and the freedom those styles implied—decided simply to stay at home. Men were also affected but not as drastically. They stopped wearing ties, which were considered signs of Western domination, and grew beards, which many traditional Muslims regard obligatory according to the sayings of Muhammad.

Forcible *hejab* was a reaction by the new Islamic government against the forcible modernization of clothing styles that had been imposed by both Pahlavi shahs. The early restrictions on clothing imposed by the revolutionaries were easier to enforce during the Iran-Iraq War because they were seen as a patriotic duty in a time of crisis. After the war ended, the strictures were gradually relaxed. For example, nail polish was again allowed, as long as it was pale. Twenty years after the revolution, Wright found that "the revolution's rigid rules relaxed enough to allow nail polish to be sold at every salon, perfumerie and department store, often in outrageous shades."[26] But the rules about clothing and makeup—and the vigor with which the rules are enforced—can change overnight in Iran. This leaves many Iranian women uncertain whether any deviation from strict *hejab* will be punished.

In accordance with the law, young women wear chadors as they walk down the street in Esfahan.

Iranian attitudes toward *hejab,* and in general about the role of women in Islam and society, are complex. For example, despite restrictions on women's roles in public life, after the revolution Ayatollah Khomeini decided that women should have the opportunity to study Islamic law in a manner similar to that of men. As a result, women's seminaries were set up, one of which was Zahra's Society in Qom, where the walls were decorated with sayings from Khomeini in praise of the role of women in the revolution.

Iranian women hold a wide range of opinions about *hejab*. One student at Zahra's Society who was interviewed by Wright said, "The revolution didn't impose religion on me. It opened up opportunities. *Hejab* doesn't limit me. It frees me to be a person judged not by beauty but by actions and thoughts. My life has been much improved, and I think my three daughters will have real opportunities."[27] Many Iranian women disagree, however, as evidenced by the fact that *hejab* rules are constantly challenged, especially in Tehran and other large cities, by women willing to risk harassment or arrest.

Iran Under Wraps

Whatever their decision regarding *hejab,* women in Iran are generally free of governmental interference in the way they behave at home. This respect for privacy has deep roots in Islam and in Iranian history and culture. For many centuries in Iran, concealment has been a way of managing conflict, a recognized and even celebrated part of Iranian culture, and it has been vitally important in the rapid political changes Iran has undergone since the late 1970s. According to journalist Elaine Sciolino:

> Concealment makes Iranians very different from Americans. Americans live in houses with front yards that face out to the street. They sit on their front porches and watch the world go by. Iranians live in houses with front gardens hidden behind high walls. There is no connection to the street life outside. It is no accident that figures in Persian miniatures are often seen peering secretly from behind balconies or curtains or half-closed doors.[28]

Working the System

In Iran, appearances can be deceiving, and many Iranians give a false impression of support for the government and its regulations in order to make their lives a little easier. In her book *Black on Black: Iran Revisited,* Ana M. Briongos records an experience in which an Iranian woman used *hejab* and feigned piety to get through customs at the Tehran airport.

> The woman behind me is strictly dressed in a black *chador.* Just as the inquisitive guard is about to open her bag, she distracts him by asking very humbly where she can find the praying area for women, because she wants to pray before embarking and doesn't know if she'll have time. Impressed by this devotion, the guard gives her careful directions, tells her she can close her bags, without even having looked at them or having asked her any questions, and wishes her well on her journey. I'm thinking: that's a good system for getting through customs in Islamic countries. Later, in the plane, I notice the same woman tucking into [eating quickly] sweets from a box. Her head is uncovered, revealing hair dyed a yellowish blonde, and the change surprises me. But when we get off the plane, it is even more surprising: tight skirt, high-heeled shoes and bright red lipstick.

One of the roots of concealment is the Shia Muslim practice of *taqiyya* or religious dissimulation, which allows those under threat of death to deny their faith and so live to fight another day. This was especially necessary during times when the Shia were being persecuted by other Muslims. There is another form of concealment, however, that is common in daily social interactions. It is known as *taarof,* and in some ways it is no different from Western politeness—telling someone you like the way their new hairstyle looks when actually you do not. In political discussions, *taarof* means that it is often difficult to determine whether someone supports a particular stand on an issue or is just expressing agreement to avoid conflict.

A more serious level of concealment, though, in which one may act against one's true beliefs in order to survive, is known in Farsi as *ketman.* According to Ana M. Briongos:

Thinking about *ketman* reminds me of a friend, Dr. Kasimi, a professor in the Faculty of Literature at the University of Tehran and the host of a cultural programme on Iranian television. Before anyone had realised the Revolution was drawing near, he used to tell me how he admired the Spanish, because although they were dominated by the Arabs for longer than Iran—eight hundred years, almost a millennium—they hadn't adopted their alphabet or converted to Islam. He was a very Iranian young man, the only son of a cultivated couple, and not in the least Westernised. . . . I have been told that after the beginning of the Revolution he appeared on television, like many other eminent Iranians, proclaiming his faith and recognising the error of his ways. I am sure he did it under duress, so as not to have to flee the country or end up in Evin, the prison on the outskirts of Tehran, from which many never returned. I thought how terrible it must have been for such a dignified man to play that role in front of the whole country, but then I remembered *ketman*: inside, Dr. Kasimi was intact, he was doing what he had to do in those circumstances, saving himself and his thought for better times.[29]

The practice of *ketman* has meant that many Iranians who appeared to support the hard-line mullahs during the 1980s were merely waiting until it was safer to voice their opposition. Perhaps the most striking evidence of this was that 70 percent of voters cast their ballots for reformers in the 2000 Majlis and 2001 presidential elections.

Sometimes, though, outright denial is not necessary. The simplest form of concealment is silence, which can be especially useful in politics. Sciolino tells the story of an Iranian she met while Khomeini was living in Paris and who rose quickly to high office after the revolution:

Hasan Habibi is emblematic of the concealer who found success in the Islamic Republic. I first met him in Paris before the revolution, when Ayatollah Khomeini was in exile in

France. Habibi said so little whenever I was with him that I didn't realize until much later that he even spoke French. Soon after the revolution he was named the spokesman for the ruling Revolutionary Council. I went to see him one evening and told him the job didn't seem like a good fit. "I am the silent spokesman," he said. "That's why they gave me the job." Twenty years later, he was a Vice President, with a big portfolio [that is, he was in charge of several government agencies] to accompany his closed mouth. [30]

The Power of the *Bazaaris*

Concealment plays a part in the way of life of a crucial element of Iranian society, the *bazaaris*—the shopkeepers, craftspeople, and others who work in the bazaars and the associated mosques in the cities of Iran. The *bazaaris* were central to the conflicts and revolutions of the twentieth century and continue to be important in the twenty-first. Many historians have pointed out that no government in Iran can last long without the support, or at least the cooperation, of the *bazaaris* who make up the economic and social heart of the cities.

Though *bazaaris* compete with one another for customers, they depend on the free flow of some kinds of information for their economic system to function properly. According to historian Roy Mottahedeh,

Two men meeting on the street meet merely as two men, but for over a thousand years the bazaar has been recognized by Islamic law as a special arena of human life, and in law as well as in common understanding two men meet there as "two men of the bazaar." As such they share certain moral and even legal obligations—for example, to buy and sell with a shared knowledge of the current market price. Information about prices is, in fact, the quickening breath that sustains the life of the bazaar, and the mechanism by which these prices adjust to new information on supply and demand is so refined as to seem almost divine. "God sets prices," according to a saying ascribed to the Prophet Mohammed. [31]

The Bazaar

In Iranian culture, the bazaar is not only a place for buying and selling goods but also for the exchange of ideas, news, and gossip, and often it has become a potent force in politics. In his book *The Mantle of the Prophet: Religion and Politics in Iran,* scholar Roy Mottahedeh explains why the bazaar is important in the political life of Iran.

When political life comes to a boil, the bazaar is not just the public assessor of values—it becomes a direct arena for political expression. At such times, in the classic Persian expression, the bazaar is "in disorder," which means that people come and go in an agitated way and seem close to violence and riot. When the bazaar boils over, it simply shuts. Streets of shop fronts barred by heavy shutters testify to the determination of merchants not to let normal life continue until the common concern is dealt with.

Moments at which the Tehran bazaar closed punctuate the last two centuries of Iranian history. In December 1905 the governor of Tehran punished two sugar merchants by the bastinado—caning on the soft soles of the feet—which is a repellant and persistent feature of Iranian penal practice. The sugar merchants were punished for not lowering their prices as ordered, although they insisted that high import prices gave them no choice. The bazaar closed. In fact the whole capital closed down, following the lead of the bazaar; unrest and dissatisfaction with the Qajar government that had been growing for years now came into the open. Many merchants and mullahs took sanctuary in nearby shrines and refused to return until the shah met their demands for some voice in the government. The first Iranian revolution had begun.

This reliance on Islamic tradition and a thousand years of mercantile custom means that in some ways *bazaaris* are staunch defenders of individual rights, especially when the government interferes in their business. The bazaars are a perfect environment for the rapid spread of news and the formation of a consensus. According to Sciolino, "The bazaar is . . . a densely built community center—with mosques, public baths, back rooms—that serves as a meeting place and center of communication. The mosque is not only a place of worship; it is also a vehicle for political mobilization."[32]

From the Constitutional Revolution of 1906 to the Islamic Revolution of 1978 and 1979, the *bazaaris,* often influenced by their mullahs, were a powerful force in national politics. Early in the twentieth century, they were able to shut down commerce at a moment's notice. Now the situation is more complex, with more shops and even large stores located outside the bazaar, and the oil industry, which has never been part of *bazaari* culture, bringing in a major portion of national revenues. But the *bazaaris* are still a force to be reckoned with in the nation's conflicts and a powerful influence in the formation of public opinion and either support or opposition for government policy.

The Hearts and Minds of the People

The *bazaaris* tend to be conservative and highly religious, so they were key supporters of the return of Ayatollah Khomeini, and their affection for him was deep and genuine. Many other Iranians shared their feelings. But Khomeini's often contradictory and ineffective approaches to the nation's problems eventually led many citizens to disagree with him, no matter how much they admired him personally. During his lifetime, though, few dared to disagree with him in public. Silence and concealment were often necessary for Iranians both inside and outside the government because dissent could be harshly punished.

The bazaar is at the center of Iranian politics and culture.

Early in the twenty-first century, however, political disagreements are more out in the open. For example, Abdolkarim Soroush, the leading reformist thinker in Iran, believes that in an Islamic state the right of a leader to rule must come from the people. He believes that Islamic governments that stay in office by force are not legitimate and that Islam should not be used as a political ideology. According to Soroush, "Religious ideology shouldn't be used to rule a modern state, because it tends toward totalitarianism. . . . And no form of government, religious or otherwise, is capable of forcibly making a people religious."[33]

The harsh and seemingly arbitrary measures sometimes used by the government of the Islamic Republic may have alienated a sizeable portion of the Iranian public. One sign that Iranians are disillusioned with their politicians is that they have stayed away from the polls—many voters abstained from the October 1998 elections for the Assembly of Experts because of increasing dissatisfaction over the extensive powers of the Supreme Leader. Ezzatollah Sahabi, the editor of the weekly *Iran-e Farda* (Iran of Tomorrow) and his staff did not vote. As he explained to Robin Wright,

> A lot of people also want to say that the [Supreme] Leader should be supervised and that all people should have a role in supervising him, not just eighty-six clerics. Since that's not an option, they're communicating by not voting. . . . The Faqih may have seemed like a good idea at first, when the Imam [Khomeini] was alive. But it's become the same as a dynasty. It's a dynasty with supernatural powers.[34]

Islam in the Islamic Republic

There is some evidence that the coercive and undemocratic tactics of the Islamic Republic have backfired not only in terms of political opposition but also in alienating the Iranian people from Islam. The mullahs that ordinary Iranians saw as their saviors when they forced the shah to leave are now seen by many as oppressors, and the practice of Islam has suffered as a result. According to Wright,

As the Islamic Republic began its third decade [in 1998], vast numbers of Iranians were indeed indifferent about an ideology that once inspired them to revolt. Public zealotry and passionate displays of piety had largely disappeared. As faith once again became a private rather than a public practice, Iran's mosques were virtually empty. Widespread complaints about the noise from mosques even forced the office of Ayatollah Khamenei to appeal to clergy throughout Iran to turn down their muezzins [loudspeakers used for the call to prayer]. [35]

Iranian exile Morteza Mohit says that Iranians are much less religious than they were before the revolution due to reaction against the restrictions placed on civil liberties by the ruling clerics. Thus, the conservatives' efforts to make Iran more Islamic in its outward aspects have made many Iranians less interested in Islam as a religion. For example, Mohit characterizes the 2000 Majlis elections as undemocratic, complaining of an atmosphere of violence and intimidation. A peaceful demonstration at Tehran University over closure of the newspaper *Salaam* was attacked by police and *hezbollahis*. Several demonstrators were killed, many were injured, and hundreds were arrested. Two of those arrested were later executed. Following the demonstrations, opposition groups were banned. The Council of Guardians disqualified eight hundred reformist candidates from running for the Majlis, and the election rules were changed so that incumbents needed only 25 percent of the vote to retain office. Mohit hints that such tactics may bring on yet another revolution. He says that there is "a broad coalition of workers, peasants, urban and rural poor, shopkeepers, government employees, writers, artists, students, and teachers who are ready to fight for their basic democratic rights." [36]

Protest Movements

More active political protest than merely refusing to vote has been seen on several fronts. In the mid-1990s, members of the arts community began to protest the restrictions the revolutionary government had placed on their freedom of expression. An open letter

A Visit to a Mosque

In her book *Honeymoon in Purdah: An Iranian Journey,* author Alison Wearing describes a visit to a mosque in Iran in which she saw what seemed to her one of the important roots of Iran's culture, the way in which Islam becomes an integral part of life for the children of devout Muslims.

The Great Mosque sits outstretched, one arch of its walls left open to a grand open-air courtyard. Persian carpets blanket the ground where hundreds upon hundreds upon hundreds of devotees stand, kneel, bow, submit. Breathe prayers to the sky.

A boy stands next to his father, stands as tall as his father's thigh, and learns the choreography of Islam. The boy tries to look stern and focused, but he is nervous, self-conscious, unsure of himself. He watches the other men out of the corner of his eye, sneaks peeks at the next move, then follows, hurriedly, a split-second late. His is a rushed, jerky dance of devotion, but it will improve. And the rhythm of this ritual will wash into his blood and live there as a lifeline. The line of his life. Something he would die for.

The Amir Chakhmaq Mosque in Yazd, Iran.

titled "We Are Writers" was composed over a ten-month period by eight of Tehran's leading intellectuals and was signed by 134 writers, reporters, teachers, and others. The letter was never published inside Iran but was broadcast by the BBC and the Voice of America and appeared in some Western publications. "We Are Writers" requested three things: the end of censorship, freedom for writers to associate with one another, and an end to interference in writers' private lives.

The government responded quickly and in a variety of ways. Many of the signers of the letter found were told that they might be fired from their jobs or that they would not be allowed to publish their writings in Iran. Some were interrogated by government agents. Ten of the signers withdrew their support within weeks of the letter's release. One of the signers said, "More of us may back down. I may even have to do or say something to keep my job. But knowledge of the letter and what it represents is now out there, and for all this government's power, it can't retract an idea." [37]

Since the beginnings of the Islamic Republic, elements of the government have thought that Western culture was damaging to the Iranian people. Conservatives in the Majlis wanted to ban VCRs because they saw such technology as dangerous to the revolution. But a compromise was struck that allowed Iranians to keep their VCRs, though the Majlis banned virtually all foreign videos and the government supplied video stores with tapes that had approved Islamic themes. Conservatives next moved to ban satellite dishes because, as Grand Ayatollah Mohammad Ali Araqi put it, they spread the "family-devastating diseases of the West." [38] After the law banning satellite dishes went into effect in 1995, dishes were confiscated and military helicopters were flown over cities in search of dishes that had been hidden in courtyards or disguised as air conditioners. But, as Ibrahim Yazdi, who had been the revolution's first foreign minister put it, "Nobody can close the sky." [39] By 1999, the ban on satellite dishes was eased so that some people active in the arts, education, the media, and government were allowed to have them at home. The

Two students protest the banning of a popular newspaper. Their mouths are taped shut to represent the loss of free expression.

head of Iran's Ministry of Culture and Islamic Guidance, Ataollah Mohajerani, said that "It's time to stop being afraid of the outside world." [40]

Another gauge of the political climate in Iran is the way movies and moviemakers are treated. The movies that are allowed to play in the theaters of Tehran can be an indication of whether the government, especially the clerical establishment and their allies in the Revolutionary Guard, are in a mood to tighten or to loosen controls. The government used to have a hand in the production process, requiring moviemakers to get script approval before they could begin shooting feature films. Now the censorship occurs later in the process—controversial films are often not allowed to be shown in theaters.

Sometimes, though, the authorities use other means to exert control. A case in point is Iranian film director Tahmineh Milani, whose 1999 film *Two Women* did well at international film festivals. In August 2001, Milani was arrested and charged with "insulting the values of the Islamic republic."[41] Her film *The Hidden Half* was showing in Tehran at the time of her arrest. After a hearing before a revolutionary court in Tehran she was taken to prison, though she was later released on bail. The fact that the film could be made and shown in the capital but then be the occasion for the director's arrest shows how the factors influencing freedom of expression fluctuate in Iran. According to Elaine Sciolino:

> The Islamic Republic is a fluid place where the rules are hard to keep straight because they keep changing. What is banned one day might be permitted the next. I've heard it said that Iranian political leaders are terrific chess players, always plotting their strategy ten steps ahead. To me they are more like players in a jazz band, changing the rhythm and the tempo and picking up spontaneous cues from each other as they go along. Knowing how to improvise is the only way to get things done—and sometimes even to survive.[42]

Crime and Punishment

At times Iran's government has also seemed to be improvising not only censorship rules but also its criminal justice system. Over the first twenty years of the Islamic Republic, what was considered a crime and how crimes were punished varied widely. In the early days, the crime most likely to result in a death sentence was being a royalist, that is, having been closely allied with the shah or advocating his return. Soon there was a new reason for the death penalty being imposed—thousands of socialists and Communists were executed in the struggle for control of the government in the early 1980s.

Historically, two forces have interacted in the Islamic Republic: the desire of many members of the Iranian public for more freedom and the desire of the clerics to maintain control. This has resulted in the clerics and their supporters closely monitoring the most visible signs of freedom, such as clothing, dancing, movies, and the press. Whether the signs of personal freedom—women wearing makeup and less than full *hejab* clothing, for example—have led to harassment and persecution has depended on how secure the clerics felt their hold on power to be.

Restrictions on the Majlis

The Majlis that was elected in 2000 was overwhelmingly committed to reform, which caused considerable conflict with Ayatollah Khamenei and his supporters. Despite this, the complex web of government branches in Iran worked to keep the Supreme Leader and other clerics in control. At the beginning of the twenty-first century, an electorate that supported a reformist president and Majlis again faced a cultural war waged by the judiciary, the Revolutionary Guards, and other groups controlled by the clerics. One of the more serious incidents was the arrest in 2001 of members of the Majlis for criticizing Iran's court system. Previously Majlis members had enjoyed immunity from prosecution for anything they said, but judiciary chief Mahmoud Hashemi Shahroudi ignored this precedent, an obvious attempt to intimidate his critics. This was one of many indications of the precarious balance in Iran between its democratic institutions and its authoritarian ruling clerics.

In 2001 Hashemi Shahroudi reinstituted harsh sentences such as public hanging for adultery and flogging for offenses as minor as attending parties where rock music was played. He was severely criticized both by international human rights organizations and by some Iranians, but he gave no indication he would revise his policies.

   Hashemi Shahroudi relied on the Revolutionary Guards to enforce his edicts. Originally recruited as bodyguards for the mullahs, the Revolutionary Guards' role quickly expanded into a full-fledged army. In recent years they have functioned as morality police, enforcing restrictions on public behavior with public lashings. Their punishments have drawn protests from many Iranians, though, indicating that the conflicts over the application of Islamic principles to Iranian society are still at the heart of the nation's unrest, as well as being a source of tension with the West.

Isolation, Crisis, and Change

5

For many decades, Iran's relationship with the West has swung in a long arc, with total isolation at one end and frantic efforts to become part of the Western world at the other. Under the Pahlavi shahs, Iran's leaders and many of its people found Western culture attractive and tried to graft it onto the Iranian way of life, but these attempts brought protests from conservative Islamic clerics and their followers. Since the Islamic Revolution, Iran's leaders have generally viewed the West as an enemy at every level—religiously, culturally, economically, and militarily—and again a portion of the population has been firmly opposed. The undemocratic nature of Iranian politics under both the shahs and the ayatollahs has meant that the positions of those in power have been extreme and intolerant of dissent, a condition that has distorted international relations in various ways.

Iran's isolation since the Islamic Revolution has been due to many factors: its history of manipulation by foreigners; the poor understanding of Islam and Iranian culture by the West and blanket denunciations of the West by some Iranians; the nationalization of the oil industry; the hostage crisis; the Iran-Iraq War and the Iran-Contra scandal; Ayatollah Khomeini's fatwa against novelist Salman Rushdie; Iran's support of terrorism and its attempts to export its revolution to other Muslim nations; and Iran's internal conflicts and instability.

The Enigma of Iran

The complexities of society and politics in the Islamic Republic are difficult to grasp even for Iranians. They are nearly impossible to comprehend for most Americans. Scholar Edward Said argues that this is partly because the United States never had any colonies with majority-Muslim populations. He says that American leaders tended to ignore Islam as a religion because it seemed to them foreign and even antagonistic. As a result, Islam was not appreciated on its own terms.

Of course, the misunderstanding is mutual. Many of Iran's leaders know little about Europe and America. In their public statements they seem to have heard only of the West's problems with drinking and drug abuse, sex and violence in movies and television, and rampant crime and corruption. Just as some in the West think that they have nothing in common with Islam and Iran, some Iranians think there is no basis for productive contact with the West. Ayatollah Khomeini frequently condemned the United States in sweeping terms, saying that its culture promoted godless materialism and sexual immorality and that its government wanted to destroy Islam.

The presence of adult bookstores and movie theaters led Ayatollah Khomeini to label American culture as godless and sexually immoral.

Khomeini also criticized America's dealings with Iran over oil and support for the shah's secret police, saying that U.S. interests were limited to whatever economic and military advantages it could wring from Iran. Khomeini used such anti-American rhetoric to forge the revolutionary coalition, and he continued to use it as he ruled the country. For example, before the April 1979 referendum on which form of government Iran would have, Khomeini said, "To achieve real independence we have to remove all forms of American influence, whether economic, political, military or cultural."[43] Khomeini's condemnations established a tradition that continued into the twenty-first century in similar pronouncements by Supreme Leader Ali Khamenei, judiciary chief Mahmoud Hashemi Shahroudi, and the head of the Expediency Council, Ali Akbar Hashemi Rafsanjani.

Not all Iranians—not even all Iranians in the government— share their leaders' anti-Western views. Many want a dialogue with the West, but most attempts to establish new lines of communication have been stopped by the hard-liners. Moreover, stable diplomatic relations require stable governments on both sides, and Iran has not been able to produce a sufficiently consistent approach to allow for sustained improvement in relations with Western nations.

A Series of Crises

The official hostility of the Islamic Republic toward the United States has been essentially continuous since the revolution. Formal diplomatic relations were severed during the hostage crisis, and then the United States became involved in the Iran-Iraq War in several ways that increased tensions between the two nations. For example, when Iran tried to blockade Iraqi shipping, the U.S. Navy destroyed two Iranian oil drilling platforms, and the United States also helped Iraq get military equipment and supplies. This U.S. support of Iraq was deeply resented by the Iranians.

In 1985, however, Hashemi Rafsanjani, who was then speaker of the Majlis, helped to free the hostages of an airliner hijacking, and this prompted U.S. officials to secretly ask for Iran's help in freeing American hostages held in Lebanon. In return, Iran would be allowed to purchase U.S. military equipment, and then the United States would pass on the proceeds from the sale to insurgents in Nicaragua known as Contras. The entire scheme was illegal under U.S. law. When word of the deal became public knowledge, many months of U.S. congressional hearings and criminal prosecutions followed, and this made improving relations with Iran politically impossible for U.S. officials.

A military accident in July 1988 led to further tensions. While on patrol in the Persian Gulf, the U.S. naval cruiser *Vincennes* mistakenly shot down an Iranian airliner, killing all 290 civilians on board. The disaster was the occasion of great grief in Iran. According to Sandra Mackey, "For days, Iranian television ran pictures of torn and charred bodies floating in the warm Gulf waters. Nonetheless, public reaction, by Iranian standards, remained amazingly muted. In the place of outrage hovered a funereal sense of helplessness, isolation, and weariness."[44]

The Iran-Iraq War ended in a negotiated settlement in 1988, but new international disputes quickly arose. For example, in 1989, Ayatollah Khomeini issued a fatwa (religious decree) calling for the execution of novelist Salman Rushdie because Khomeini thought Rushdie's book *The Satanic Verses,* "which had fictional dream sequences attributed to the prophet Mohammad, was blasphemous against Islam and all Muslims. Ayatollah Khomeini's death sentence froze rapprochement [improved relations] with the outside world."[45] Khomeini's fatwa further soured relations between Iran and Britain because Rushdie was a British citizen, and it angered leaders in the Muslim world as well—forty-four of forty-five member nations of the Organization of the Islamic Conference condemned Khomeini's actions.

In the 1990s, evidence that elements of the Iranian government were supporting international terrorism resulted in U.S. legislation banning all trade and investment in Iran. The ban was renewed in 2001 despite the opposition of other Western countries. A major issue in the congressional debate over sanctions was Iran's role in the bombing of Khobar Towers, a U.S. military barracks near Dhahran, Saudi Arabia. The barracks were attacked in

A Memorial at Sea

In July 1988, just weeks before the end of the Iran-Iraq War, the U.S. Navy vessel *Vincennes* mistook an Iran Air passenger jet for a hostile military aircraft and shot it down, killing all 290 passengers and crew on board. Each year a memorial service is held at sea for the victims, which is a prime opportunity for anti-American speeches. But in her book *Persian Mirrors: The Elusive Face of Iran,* journalist Elaine Sciolino illustrates just how conflicted Iranians are toward Americans.

> I went along one year, and a group of young women in chadors, whose relatives died in the crash, discovered that I was an American. But instead of venting anger, they shyly touched me and wanted to have their pictures taken with me. I was the first American they had ever met, and they were endlessly curious. Did I like Iran? What did I think of the covering that women have to wear in the breathtaking heat? They thrust pages from their notebooks and pieces of Kleenex at me. They wanted my autograph.

Iranians honor the victims of an Iran Air passenger jet that was mistakenly shot down by the U.S. Navy.

June 1996, killing nineteen U.S. personnel. In June 2001 thirteen Saudis and one Lebanese were indicted for the bombing. Although the indictment cited the prosecutors' suspicions that Iranians were involved, none were named. Some experts speculate that the bombers may have had help from lower-level Iranian officials who acted without government approval. In any case, even the suspicion that Iran might have been involved was a factor in the decision by the U.S. Congress to extend sanctions until 2006.

Iran's Response to Terrorism

Iran's responses to the terrorist attacks on the United States on September 11, 2001, expressed outrage and opposition to terrorism. In the days following the attacks, the mayors of both Tehran and Esfahan sent messages of condolence to New York mayor Rudolph Giuliani. The message from Esfahan's mayor said, "We condemn the violent and savage attacks which led to the death of thousands of innocent people. Undoubtedly, these violent acts are a threat to world peace and contrary to human interests."[46]

The Iranian government's initial stance toward the terrorist attacks on New York and Washington, D.C., was one of condemnation for the terrorists and sympathy for their victims. Only hours after the attack, both President Khatami and Supreme Leader Khamenei condemned it, and Khatami called for international resolve to combat terrorism. At a military parade marking the twenty-first anniversary of the beginning of the Iran-Iraq War on September 22, 2001, Khatami said, "We should stir an international resolve to fight terrorism, based on the important principle that people and nations have a right to live safely in their lands."[47] And 165 members of Iran's 290-member Majlis signed a petition expressing sympathy for the United States and condoning a United Nations–led campaign against terrorism.

Still, many observers doubt that the sympathy in Iran for terrorist victims in the United States will lead to reconciliation between the two countries. As the threat of military action against the Taliban in neighboring Afghanistan grew in the fall of 2001, Iran attempted to seal its 590-mile border with Afghanistan so that it

*Smoke fills the sky over New York City on September 11, 2001.
The Iranian government condemned the terrorist attacks on
the United States.*

could better control the flow of refugees. At the same time, Iran
warned the United States that military attacks on Afghanistan
could lead to a humanitarian disaster. President Khatami said, "The
government and nation of Iran understands America's situation in
the wake of the recent incidents . . . but one should not respond to
a great catastrophe by causing another."[48] In late September 2001,
Iran pledged to cooperate with world agencies to shelter refugees
near the border with Afghanistan and set up eight camps to house
the nearly two hundred thousand refugees who had already fled
Afghanistan in anticipation of U.S. military action.

Although Iran announced its willingness to cooperate in com-
bating terrorism, it also made it clear that it would not allow U.S.
planes to use its airspace to attack Afghanistan. That stance only
hardened after the United States renewed its accusations that Iran
had sponsored terrorism through its support for Lebanon's Hezbol-
lah and militant Palestinian groups such as Hamas and Islamic Ji-
had. Ayatollah Khamenei reacted with anger to the accusation of
sponsoring terrorism and reiterated his position that his country
would not provide help to U.S. military operations in Afghanistan,

saying, "Iran will not participate in any move under U.S. leadership. Iran will not extend any assistance to the U.S." [49] for its operations in Afghanistan. Nevertheless, in early 2002 there were press reports that U.S. and Iranian troops had participated in some joint missions against the Taliban in western Afghanistan.

Iran and the United States

The rhetoric on both sides regarding terrorism is just one aspect of the intense and varied relationship between Iran and the United States. According to journalist Elaine Sciolino,

> the United States remains a fantasy Promised Land for many Iranians, the land of *Baywatch* and billionaires and an easy life in Los Angeles, where hundreds of thousands of Iranians have settled. . . .
>
> Almost every Iranian I have ever met has a relative living in the United States. And even those Iranians who rail most about American policy seem to genuinely like Americans. At the height of the American embassy seizure in 1979 and 1980, the same Iranian demonstrators who chanted angry slogans about the "den of spies" in the mornings followed me down Ferdowsi Avenue in the afternoons asking me to help them get visas or contact their relatives in Los Angeles or Dallas. [50]

Iran's reform-minded president Muhammad Khatami has made several moves toward better relations with the outside world. In 1998, Khatami attended the opening session of the United Nations General Assembly, where he spoke of "replacing hostility and confrontation with discourse and understanding." [51] But the most significant obstacle to improved relations between Iran and the United States seemed to be mutual distrust. Foreign minister Kamal Kharrazi indicated in June 2001 that American actions, such as maintaining economic sanctions against Iran, using its influence against Iran at the World Bank and the World Trade Organization, and criticizing Iran's human rights record provide ample reason to distrust his nation's former ally. According to Moshen Aminzadeh, a colleague of Kharrazi's, improved relations with the United States "depend on the actions and behavior of the U.S. government."[52] In other words, Iranian officials wanted the United States to take further steps, such as loosening trade and financial restrictions, as a sign of good faith. Following the terrorist attacks of September 11, 2001, Kharrazi reiterated this position: "Once Washington's hostile policies towards Tehran are changed, and Washington takes the initiative to establish relations based on mutual respect and equality, then Tehran will be ready to review its (now-frozen) ties with the U.S."[53]

On the other hand, there is evidence that ordinary Iranians are becoming bolder in expressing their interest in better relations with the United States. In 2001 there were scattered street demonstrations in Iran in support of closer ties with the United States, and some members of the Majlis called for reestablishing formal diplomatic relations. And there are more subtle signs of détente, such as the reopening of a Coca-Cola plant in the Iranian city of Mashhad—Coca-Cola was formerly banned by the Islamic Republic along with other products considered to be symbols of American imperialism.

Like so many aspects of life in Iran, the nation's relationship with the United States is full of contradictions because of the conflict in the government between conservatives and reformers, between what officials say in public versus what they do behind the scenes, and between official policy in the Iranian capital, Tehran, versus what actually happens hundreds of miles away in the provinces. Few veteran observers of Iran find it odd that Ayatollah Khamenei would vow publicly that Iran would not cooperate in any way with American military action and then allow some joint operations or that Hashemi Shahroudi would denounce American culture at the same time Coca-Cola is allowed back into Iranian stores.

Relations with Neighboring Countries

Iranian hard-liners have often viewed neighboring Muslim countries with arrogance and superiority, believing that their form of

Iranian women wear Western clothes and dance to Western music at a private party, a sign of easing restrictions in Iran.

government is the only one genuinely based on Islamic principles. However strongly they believe that, they have had to change their policies toward other nations in the region in the face of economic stagnation and security threats. Deputy Foreign Minister Aminzadeh said in June 2001 that in the new global era, "We are in need of relations with other countries."[54] For example, despite the fact that Egypt allowed the deposed Muhammad Reza Shah Pahlavi to take refuge there after the revolution—a move condemned at the time by the Islamic Republic—the two countries have recently worked out a schedule for repayment to Iran of money Egypt has owed since before the Islamic Revolution.

Another top priority for Iran has been improving its relationship with Saudi Arabia. Ayatollah Khomeini once predicted that Iran would never forgive Saudi Arabia for supporting Iraq during the Iran-Iraq War. But the two countries reached a degree of reconciliation in the late 1990s, as evidenced by the fact that Iranian and Saudi leaders consulted with one another on topics such as their common use of Persian Gulf shipping lanes and oil production. The two countries have also signed a security pact aimed at fighting crime, terrorism, and drug trafficking.

In May 2001, Iranian and Turkish officials also signed a security agreement, demonstrating that relations between the two countries are improving. In the past Iran has condemned Turkey,

---

"Stand Firm Against the Superpowers"

The ideas behind Iran's isolation from other nations can be seen clearly in the writings of Ayatollah Khomeini. In his No Ruz (Persian New Year) message for 1980, he expressed his view that both the West, led by the United States, and the Soviet Union were the enemies of Iran and that Iran should try to incite revolutions similar to its own in other Muslim countries. Khomeini's address is quoted in *Islam and Revolution: Writings and Declarations of Imam Khomeini, 1941–1980,* translated and edited by Hamid Algar.

> God Almighty has willed—and all thanks are due to Him—that this noble nation be delivered from the oppression and crimes inflicted on it by a tyrannical government and from the domination of the oppressive powers, especially America, the global plunderer, and that the flag of Islamic justice wave over our beloved land. It is our duty to stand firm against the superpowers, as we indeed are able to do, on condition that the intellectuals stop following and imitating either the West or the East, and adhere instead to the straight path of Islam and the nation. We are at war with international communism no less than we are struggling against the global plunderers of the West. . . .

> We must strive to export our Revolution throughout the world, and must abandon all idea of not doing so, for not only does Islam refuse to recognize any difference between Muslim countries, it is the champion of all oppressed people. Moreover, all the powers are intent on destroying us, and if we remain surrounded in a closed circle, we shall certainly be defeated. We must make plain our stance toward the powers and the superpowers and demonstrate to them that despite the arduous problems that burden us, our attitude to the world is dictated by our beliefs.

which is predominantly Sunni Muslim, for being corrupted by secularism and for its relations with the United States and Israel. Iran's natural gas industry and its Caspian Sea oil reserves have helped to improve relations between Iran and Turkey. In 1996 the two countries signed a $23-billion, twenty-three-year agreement in which Turkey will buy Iranian oil. A natural gas pipeline stretches from Tabriz in Iran to Turkey's capital, Ankara. It was under construction in 2001, and by 2005 it is expected to be operating at full capacity, pumping 10 billion cubic meters a year. This is good news for Iran, whose main exports are oil and natural gas and whose economy would be boosted by the expanded capacity.

Iran's handling of a dispute with the United Arab Emirates (UAE) over ownership of three small islands in the Persian Gulf is another indication that it is more interested in reestablishing friendly ties with the outside world. The islands hold strategic importance to both Iran and the UAE because of their location near key shipping lanes through which one-fifth of the world's oil passes. Known as Abu Musa, Greater Tunb, and Lesser Tunb, the islands are occupied by Iran but are also claimed by the UAE. Following President Khatami's reelection in June 2001, the Iranian government began working on a plan to give up control of the islands if the UAE and other Gulf countries sign joint security agreements with Iran. The security agreements include a pledge not to allow any foreign military, especially the U.S. military, to maintain a presence in the Gulf and to refer to the Gulf as the Persian Gulf rather than the Arab Gulf. The security agreements could signal a new chapter in Iran's relations with the UAE as well as the other Gulf nations, though they also indicate a continuing distrust of American intentions in the region.

The Caspian Sea is another issue over which Iran has demonstrated willingness to cooperate peacefully with its neighbors. The Caspian Sea reportedly lies atop the largest pool of oil on the planet, with potential oil and gas reserves worth an estimated $4 trillion. Five countries, including Iran, border the Caspian, and ownership of its rich undersea resources is often in dispute. For example, in July 2001 an Iranian gunboat ordered two survey ships operated by the British oil company BP to leave an area of the Caspian that Iran sees as Iranian territory and Azerbaijan sees as Azeri territory. The government of Azerbaijan, Iran's neighbor to the north, protested the incident because it had given BP a license to explore the area in dispute.

But Iran expressed a desire to negotiate a peaceful settlement of the issue with Azerbaijan. Iranian foreign minister Kamal Kharrazi said that the two countries should view the Caspian as "an area of friendship and peace."[55] Kharrazi visited Azeri president Haydar Aliyev a few days after the incident, and a statement released by Aliyev's press office after the meeting said, "They decided all issues with regard to the relationship between Azerbaijan and Iran should be resolved through negotiation."[56]

Iran and Europe

The international effort to find those responsible for the terrorist attacks of September 11 presented Iran with an unprecedented opportunity to improve its relations with Europe. British prime minister Tony Blair spoke by telephone with President Khatami following the terrorist attacks, leading within days to a Tehran visit by British foreign minister Jack Straw. Straw met with his Iranian counterpart, Kamal Kharrazi, the first time a British foreign minister had traveled to the Islamic Republic since the revolution, although Britain restored diplomatic relations with Iran in 1998.

During Straw's visit, he and Kharrazi discussed British-Iranian relations, the terrorist attacks on the United States, human rights, and regional issues. Kharrazi said Iran wanted to expand cooperation with Britain based on a mutual respect for each other's values and principles. Straw asked Kharrazi's advice on Afghanistan, saying that Iran was an important source of information on Afghanistan and the Taliban rulers there. Straw also assured Iranian officials that Britain was prepared to share in confidence the evidence it had against the suspected terrorists, including Osama bin Laden, in an effort to convince the Iranians that military action in Afghanistan, where bin Laden was thought to be hiding, was justified.

Reza Pahlavi and the Next Revolution

One surprising development in 2001 was the emergence of the last shah's son, Reza Pahlavi, as a spokesman for the secular resistance in Iran. Born in 1960, Pahlavi followed his father into exile in 1979. Following the shah's death in 1980, Pahlavi proclaimed himself shah but, of course, he has had no opportunity to rule. He lost all of his inheritance from his father due to a swindle by his investment manager, and Pahlavi eventually moved to the United States.

In 2001, more Iranians became convinced that President Khatami's vision of an Islamic democracy was impossible under the current system, and they increasingly turned to Pahlavi as the only viable leader of a new—though not necessarily violent—revolution. Pahlavi advocates writing a new constitution for a secular democracy, with or without him as monarch, and submitting this to a referendum. The problem, though, is getting the ruling clerics to agree. How that might come about is highly uncertain. In an article in the January 10, 2002, *Washington Post,* Pahlavi explained his view of the situation in Iran.

> In no uncertain terms, the 50 million youth of Iran want secularism, freedom, economic opportunity and modernity. They have come to the painful realization that a prerequisite for attaining these goals is a complete change of regime. Our world has witnessed the dawn of new democracies, brought about by successful nonviolent civil disobedience and mass resistance movements from Africa to Latin America and through Eastern Europe. Let there be no doubt that Iranians thirst for the same chance to restore their unalienable right to self-determination, thus restoring the civility, dignity, tolerance and sovereignty for which the land of Persians was known for so many centuries.

The Belgian foreign minister, Louis Michel, also visited Tehran after the terrorist attacks. Meeting with Kharrazi the day after Straw's historic visit, Michel conveyed a message of friendship to the Islamic Republic and called for continued contact between Iranian and European officials on current developments. Belgium held the presidency of the European Union (EU), and Michel said during his meeting with Kharrazi that the EU wanted to promote ties with the Islamic Republic by signing trade and commercial agreements. Michel also said that because of the key role Iran plays in the region, Iran's stances on recent developments following the terrorist attacks were of prime importance to the European states.

Kharrazi welcomed the expansion of ties with the EU, particularly in the areas of technology, industry, and the private sector, though Kharrazi stressed to Michel that military actions in Afghanistan might be opposed throughout the Muslim world. However, he had earlier promised Straw, "Iran will cooperate in the fight against terrorism as part of an international effort and under the auspices of the United Nations."[57]

The Prospects for Change

Any generalization about Iran is easy to contradict. The Islamic Republic has many characteristics of a dictatorship, but it also has a long history of vigorous debate, protest, and change. Its large educated population tends to want more openness toward Europe and America and the economic progress and political freedom this implies; yet the government has closed many dissenting newspapers, quashed protest demonstrations, kept reformist politicians from running for office, and jailed Majlis members who criticized the nation's Islamic courts. But peaceful protest and dissent continue, with a lively and ever-changing debate going on in the bazaars and living rooms—and sometimes in the streets—of Tehran and other Iranian cities. The conservative clerics seem to have a stranglehold on the government, but many Iranians predict that the days of the Islamic Republic are numbered. There is even a movement that is apparently growing both within Iran and among Iranians in the West to replace the current system with a secular democracy headed by Reza Pahlavi, the son of Muhammad Reza Shah Pahlavi.

Solving the nation's many economic, political, and diplomatic problems—including the question of whether the Islamic Republic will survive or be replaced by a new government—will continue to challenge the people of Iran in the coming decades.

Notes

Introduction: The Changing Face of Iran

1. Robin Wright, *The Last Great Revolution: Turmoil and Transformation in Iran.* New York: Vintage Books, 2001, p. 8.

2. Sandra Mackey, *The Iranians: Persia, Islam, and the Soul of a Nation.* New York: Plume Books, 1996, p. xix.

Chapter One: Iran Before the Islamic Revolution

3. Pat Yale, Anthony Ham, and Paul Greenway, *Iran.* Oakland, CA: Lonely Planet Publications, 2001, p. 15.

4. John L. Esposito, *Islam: The Straight Path,* 3rd ed. New York: Oxford University Press, 1998, p. 4.

5. Mackey, *The Iranians,* p. 85.

6. Roy Mottahedeh, *The Mantle of the Prophet: Religion and Politics in Iran.* Oxford, UK: Oneworld Publications, 2000, p. 60.

7. Baqer Moin, *Khomeini: Life of the Ayatollah.* New York: St. Martin's Press, 1999, p. 64.

8. Quoted in Moin, *Khomeini,* p. 75.

9. Moin, *Khomeini,* p. 175.

10. Moin, *Khomeini,* p. 179.

11. Quoted in Moin, *Khomeini,* p. 184.

12. Quoted in Moin, *Khomeini,* p. 186.

13. Moin, *Khomeini,* pp. 195–96.

Chapter Two: The Islamic Republic of Iran

14. Ana M. Briongos, *Black on Black: Iran Revisited.* Oakland, CA: Lonely Planet Publications, 2000, p. 151.

15. Moin, *Khomeini,* p. 200.

16. Quoted in Moin, *Khomeini,* p. 200.

17. Quoted in Massoumeh Ebtekar and Fred A. Reed, *Takeover in Tehran: The Inside Story of the 1979 U.S. Embassy Capture.* Vancouver, Canada: Talonbooks, 2000, p. 119.

18. John Simpson and Tira Shubart, *Lifting the Veil: Life in Revolutionary Iran.* London: Hodder and Stoughton, 1995, pp. 287–88.

19. NetIran, "The Legislative." www.netiran.com.

Chapter Three: Chronic Instability
20. Mottahedeh, *The Mantle of the Prophet,* p. 51.

21. Quoted in Mottahedeh, *The Mantle of the Prophet,* p. 52.

22. Mackey, *The Iranians,* p. 179.

23. Mackey, *The Iranians,* p. 303.

24. Mackey, *The Iranians,* p. 306.

Chapter Four: A Society in Conflict
25. Wright, *The Last Great Revolution,* p. xii.

26. Wright, *The Last Great Revolution,* p. xx.

27. Quoted in Wright, *The Last Great Revolution,* p. 155.

28. Elaine Sciolino, *Persian Mirrors: The Elusive Face of Iran.* New York: Free Press, 2000, pp. 29–30.

29. Briongos, *Black on Black,* p. 93.

30. Sciolino, *Persian Mirrors,* p. 30.

31. Mottahedeh, *The Mantle of the Prophet,* pp. 34–35.

32. Sciolino, *Persian Mirrors,* pp. 29–30.

33. Quoted in Wright, *The Last Great Revolution,* p. 55.

34. Quoted in Wright, *The Last Great Revolution,* p. 73.

35. Wright, *The Last Great Revolution,* p. 28.

36. Morteza Mohit, "Background to the Parliamentary Election in Iran," *Monthly Review,* March 2000, p. 20.

37. Quoted in Wright, *The Last Great Revolution,* p. 95.

38. Quoted in Wright, *The Last Great Revolution,* p. 88.

39. Quoted in Wright, *The Last Great Revolution,* p. 89.

40. Quoted in Wright, *The Last Great Revolution,* p. 117.

41. Quoted in Modher Amin, "Iranian Female Movie Director Arrested," United Press International, August 30, 2001.

42. Sciolino, *Persian Mirrors,* pp. 30–31.

Chapter Five: Isolation, Crisis, and Change

43. Quoted in Moin, *Khomeini,* p. 213.

44. Mackey, *The Iranians,* p. 331.

45. Wright, *The Last Great Revolution,* p. 20.

46. Quoted in Reuters, "Iran Moves to Shape Clear Policy on Terrorism," September 22, 2001.

47. Quoted in Reuters, "Iran Moves to Shape Clear Policy on Terrorism."

48. Quoted in Jon Hemming, "Britain, Iran Trade Ideas on Tackling Terrorism," Reuters, September 25, 2001.

49. Quoted in Ali Akbar Dareini, "Iran Won't Help U.S.," Associated Press, September 26, 2001.

50. Sciolino, *Persian Mirrors,* pp. 44–45.

51. Quoted in Wright, *The Last Great Revolution,* p. 66.

52. Quoted in Cameron W. Barr, "Iran Finds a Little Diplomacy Goes a Long Way: Global Era Turns Foes into Friends," *Washington Times,* June 20, 2001, p. A14.

53. Quoted in Islamic Republic News Agency, "Straw Describes Meeting with Kharrazi 'Historic,'" September 25, 2001. www.irna.com.

54. Quoted in Barr, "Iran Finds a Little Diplomacy Goes a Long Way," p. A14.

55. Quoted in Reuters, "Iran Welcomes Azeri Call for Talks on Caspian Row," July 21, 2001.

56. Quoted in Reuters, "Iran Welcomes Azeri Call for Talks on Caspian Row."

57. Quoted in Jon Hemming, "Iran Stays in Regular Contact with U.S. on Terrorism," Reuters, September 23, 2001.

Chronology

B.C.
559–330
Achaemenian dynasty rules the Persian Empire.

334–190
Persia is invaded and eventually conquered and ruled by
Alexander the Great and his successors, the Seleucid dynasty.

190– A.D. 224
Persia is ruled by the Parthian dynasty.

A.D.
224–637
The Sassanid dynasty rules Persia; Zoroastrianism is the official religion.

651
Arab Muslims assassinate Sassanid emperor Yazdgard III,
completing the Islamic conquest of Persia.

1051–1220
Seljuk Turks gain control of Persia.

1220–1380
Mongol tribes invade Persia, destroying cities and massacring
inhabitants.

1501–1722
The Safavid dynasty rules Persia, declaring Shia Islam the state
religion.

1794–1925
The Qajar dynasty rules Persia.

1906–1911
The Constitutional Revolution leads to a new constitution limiting royal power.

1921

Persian Cossack Brigade officer Reza Khan defeats rival leaders and takes control in Tehran.

1925

The Qajar shah is officially deposed; Reza Khan becomes Reza Shah Pahlavi.

1935

The shah changes the country's name to Iran.

1941

Reza Shah Pahlavi abdicates in favor of his son, Muhammad Reza Shah Pahlavi.

1944

Reza Shah Pahlavi dies.

1953

Prime Minister Muhammad Mosaddeq nationalizes the oil industry; he is later removed from office in a coup.

1961

The shah dissolves the Majlis.

1979

In January the shah flees Iran amid growing opposition; in February, Ayatollah Khomeini returns from exile; in April, Iranians vote to establish the Islamic Republic of Iran; in October, the physically ailing shah is allowed to enter the United States.

1979–1981

The hostage crisis begins on November 4, 1979, when Iranian students seize the U.S. embassy in Tehran and hold more than fifty U.S. citizens hostage for 444 days.

1980–1988

The Iran-Iraq War devastates Iran's economy, destroys several towns and hundreds of villages, with up to a million Iranian casualties.

1989

Ayatollah Khomeini dies in June and is succeeded by Ayatollah Khamenei; Ali Akbar Hashemi Rafsanjani is elected president; constitutional revisions are affirmed in a referendum.

1997
Muhammad Khatami is elected president.

2000
In the Majlis elections, many reformist candidates are elected.

2001
Khatami is reelected president.

For Further Reading

Books

Manucher Farmanfarmaian and Roxane Farmanfarmaian, *Blood and Oil: Inside the Shah's Iran.* New York: Modern Library, 1997. This book gives the inside story of Iran's oil industry and the political intrigues surrounding it during the reign of the last shah.

Cyrus Ghani, *Iran and the Rise of Reza Shah: From Qajar Collapse to Pahlavi Rule.* London: I.B. Tauris, 1998. An examination of the transition from the Qajar dynasty to the consolidation of power by Reza Shah Pahlavi.

Dilip Hiro, *The Longest War: The Iran-Iraq Military Conflict.* New York: Routledge, 1991. One of the standard accounts of the Iran-Iraq War.

Paul H. Kreisberg, ed., *American Hostages in Iran: The Conduct of a Crisis.* New Haven, CT: Yale University Press, 1985. With each chapter written by a different authority, this book gives a comprehensive inside account of the U.S. government's handling of the hostage crisis.

Daniel Ladinsky, trans., *The Gift: Poems by Hafiz, the Great Sufi Master.* New York: Penguin, 1999. This is one of many modern English translations of the poet who was not only Khomeini's favorite but also a major influence on many poets and thinkers in the Islamic world and the West.

Robert D. McFadden et al., *No Hiding Place.* New York: Times Books, 1981. Based on interviews by the *New York Times* with the Americans who were held hostage in Iran from 1979 to 1981, this book gives the inside story of the hostage crisis.

Maria O'Shea, *Iran: A Guide to Customs and Etiquette.* Portland, OR: Graphic Arts Center, 1999. An explanation of the complexities of the society and customs of the Islamic Republic.

Gary Sick, *All Fall Down: America's Tragic Encounter with Iran.* New York: Penguin, 1986. Written by a senior American official, this book focuses on the Iran hostage crisis of 1979 to 1981.

Lawrence E. Walsh, *Firewall: The Iran-Contra Conspiracy and Cover-Up.* New York: W.W. Norton, 1997. The author, who was the independent counsel in the Iran-Contra investigation, explains the cover-up that pervaded all levels of the Reagan administration.

Walter M. Weiss, *Islam: An Illustrated Historical Overview.* Hauppauge, NY: Barron's, 2000. A book designed for travelers going to Muslim countries for the first time, it is well organized and clearly written.

Websites

Islamic Republic News Agency (www.irna.com). The official news source of the Islamic Republic.

NetIran (www.netiran.com). The official English-language website of the government of Iran.

Salam Iran (www.salamiran.org). A website operated by the Iranian embassy in Ottawa, Ontario, Canada.

Tehran Times (www.tehrantimes.com). A daily news source covering internal politics, international affairs, cultural events, and sports.

Works Consulted

Books

Abol Hassan Bani-Sadr, *My Turn to Speak: Iran, the Revolution and Secret Deals with the U.S.* Washington, DC: Brassey's, 1991. This is an account of the Islamic Revolution written by the first president of the Islamic Republic.

Christiane Bird, *Neither East nor West: One Woman's Journey Through the Islamic Republic of Iran.* New York: Pocket Books, 2001. The author, who traveled alone through the Islamic Republic in the late 1990s, gives an account of the country and people she encountered on her journey.

Ana M. Briongos, *Black on Black: Iran Revisited.* Oakland, CA: Lonely Planet Publications, 2000. The author is a Spanish woman who has traveled and studied extensively in Iran.

Daniel Brumberg, *Reinventing Khomeini: The Struggle for Reform in Iran.* Chicago: University of Chicago Press, 2001. This book chronicles Iran's struggles to become a democracy after the revolution.

Massoumeh Ebtekar and Fred A. Reed, *Takeover in Tehran: The Inside Story of the 1979 U.S. Embassy Capture.* Vancouver, Canada: Talonbooks, 2000. A narrative of the hostage crisis by one of the students who seized the embassy (Ebtekar), who went on to head the Iranian Department of the Environment in the 1990s.

John L. Esposito, *Islam: The Straight Path.* 3rd ed. New York: Oxford University Press, 1998. Written by a well-known scholar, this is one of the standard introductions to Islam.

Erika Friedl, *Women of Deh Koh: Lives in an Iranian Village.* New York: Penguin, 1991. A discussion of the issues confronting women in the Islamic Republic of Iran, especially those who live outside the major cities.

Ruhollah Khomeini, *Islam and Revolution: Writings and Declarations of Imam Khomeini, 1941–1980.* Trans. Hamid Algar. Berkeley, CA: Mizan Press, 1981. A collection of Khomeini's books, pamphlets, sermons, and speeches mainly from the decade preceding the revolution.

Sandra Mackey, *The Iranians: Persia, Islam, and the Soul of a Nation.* New York: Plume Books, 1996. The author shows how the relationship between Iran's Persian and Islamic heritage affects the way Iranians see themselves today.

Helen Chapin Metz, ed., *Iran: A Country Study.* Washington, DC: Library of Congress, 1989. Although somewhat dated, this book remains an excellent source for the history and geography of Iran.

Baqer Moin, *Khomeini: Life of the Ayatollah.* New York: St. Martin's Press, 1999. This biography covers the life and times of Iran's first Supreme Leader.

Moojan Momen, *An Introduction to Shi'i Islam: The History and Doctrines of Twelver Shi'ism.* New Haven, CT: Yale University Press, 1985. A clear and detailed description of Shii Islam, especially as it is practiced in Iran.

Roy Mottahedeh, *The Mantle of the Prophet: Religion and Politics in Iran.* Oxford, UK: Oneworld Publications, 2000. This account of Islam and politics in revolutionary Iran is drawn from eyewitness accounts of the events since the 1979 revolution.

A.T. Olmstead, *History of the Persian Empire.* Chicago: University of Chicago Press, 1948. This is one of the standard histories of ancient Persia.

Taj al-Saltana, *Crowning Anguish: Memoirs of a Persian Princess from the Harem to Modernity, 1884–1914.* Washington, DC: Mage Publishers, 1993. This book offers a historical sketch by the daughter of one of the last Qajar rulers of Iran.

Elaine Sciolino, *Persian Mirrors: The Elusive Face of Iran.* New York: Free Press, 2000. The author provides an in-depth look at conditions in postrevolutionary Iran.

John Simpson and Tira Shubart, *Lifting the Veil: Life in Revolutionary Iran.* London: Hodder and Stoughton, 1995. One of the best accounts of life in Iran in the early 1990s.

Alison Wearing, *Honeymoon in Purdah: An Iranian Journey.* New York: Picador USA, 2000. A young Canadian woman writes about her experiences with the fascinating people she met while traveling through the Islamic Republic.

Robin Wright, *The Last Great Revolution: Turmoil and Transformation in Iran.* New York: Vintage Books, 2001. The author, an American journalist, examines the multitude of changes in the Islamic Republic during the first two decades after the revolution.

Pat Yale, Anthony Ham, and Paul Greenway, *Iran.* Oakland, CA: Lonely Planet Publications, 2001. This guidebook offers extensive information on topics such as the history, architecture, society, and conduct in Iran.

Periodicals

Modher Amin, "Iranian Female Movie Director Arrested," United Press International, August 30, 2001.

Cameron W. Barr, "Iran Finds a Little Diplomacy Goes a Long Way: Global Era Turns Foes into Friends," *Washington Times,* June 20, 2001.

Ali Akbar Dareini, "Iran Won't Help U.S.," Associated Press, September 26, 2001.

Franklin Foer, "Reza Pahlavi's Next Revolution," *New Republic,* January 14, 2002.

Jon Hemming, "Britain, Iran Trade Ideas on Tackling Terrorism," Reuters, September 25, 2001.

——, "Iran Stays in Regular Contact with U.S. on Terrorism," Reuters, September 23, 2001.

Morteza Mohit, "Background to the Parliamentary Election in Iran," *Monthly Review,* March 2000.

Reza Pahlavi, "Beyond Khatami—Freedom for Iran," *Washington Post,* January 10, 2002.

Reuters, "Iran Moves to Shape Clear Policy on Terrorism," September 22, 2001.

——, "Iran Welcomes Azeri Call for Talks on Caspian Row," July 21, 2001.

——, "UAE Determined to Win Back Iran-Held Islands," February 25, 2001.

USA Today, "Iranians Starting to Like America," January 3, 2002.

Internet Sources

Islamic Republic News Agency, "Straw Describes Meeting with Kharrazi 'Historic,'" September 25, 2001, www.irna.com.

NetIran, "Ayatollah Seyed Ali Khamenei, the Leader of the Islamic Revolution," www.netiran.com.

——, "The Legislative," www.netiran.com.

Index

Picture Credits

Cover photo: © David and Peter Turnley/CORBIS

Associated Press, AP, 42, 55, 58, 63, 74, 82, 84

© Bettmann/CORBIS, 20, 38, 79

© CORBIS, 33

© Hulton/Archive by Getty Images, 26, 29, 40, 49, 57

North Wind Picture Archives, 13

© SEF/Art Resource, NY, 19

© Arthur Thevenart/CORBIS, 72

© David and Peter Turnley/CORBIS, 87

© Roger Wood/CORBIS, 69

About the Author

Charles Clark is a freelance writer and editor who lives in Georgia.